LIVE
LAGOM

LIVE
LAGOM

BALANCED LIVING,
THE SWEDISH WAY

ANNA BRONES

TEN SPEED PRESS
California | New York

CONTENTS

INTRODUCTION   9

LAGOM AT WORK   41

LAGOM AT HOME   75

LAGOM FOR HEALTH   173

LAGOM AND THE ENVIRONMENT   189

THE LESSONS OF LAGOM   217

RESOURCES/BIBLIOGRAPHY   220

ACKNOWLEDGMENTS   221

INTRODUCTION

Sweden is a land of extremes. In the winter darkness feels everlasting, yet in the height of summer the sun barely sets. Dense, scarcely populated forests are home to lakes surrounded by granite rocks. Even in the cosmopolitan areas nature is never far away. Yet in these extremes there is a balance, a path through the middle that takes inspiration from the Swedish climate and environment. On the coldest days, warm candles flicker in a kitchen window; a welcoming scene in contrast to the stark landscape outside. Summer is a celebration, a time to release the darkness of the rest of the year, and life flourishes. This Nordic land is a country of calming hues, the pale grays and blues of the rocks and sky easing into warm yellows of the sun streaming into a living room. Buildings are orderly, functional, their design an expression of the culture that has brought them to life.

Whether we've spent time in Sweden or not, we are most likely familiar with this Scandinavian country, partial to some of these scenes. For many, there is an allure to Sweden, and while its population is small, its cultural influence is significant. Without even having travelled there, we feel like we know the Swedes. We've listened to their music, read their books, tasted their food, been inspired by their design. There is a love and respect for Swedish culture, often admiration, even for those who aren't affiliated by family connection or haven't stepped foot into the country.

Culturally, Sweden is often put on a pedestal, the place we sometimes dream of living, the place we look to for lessons on how to live. Like its Scandinavian counterparts, it's a country where the quality of living is high, people are treated equally and nature is respected and revered. The country is regularly among the top players in lists of best places to live—for social health, happiness, sustainability, and beyond—giving economists and political scientists renewed reason to look to the Nordic Model.

From the outside looking in, Swedish culture exudes a general calmness and order. Things rarely seem to be out of place, with no room for chaos. The most visual representation of this is Scandinavian design. Simple and

pared down, the country's most well-known designs speak to a need for function and aesthetic. Even in the wilder colors and prints to be found in iconic Swedish textiles, there is a general sense of rationality; never too much to leave you feeling overwhelmed, just enough to keep you interested.

In a chaotic, modern world, this all feels like a breath of fresh air. We're craving more balance, more equality, more simplicity. We're looking for something that's often hard to put an exact name to, but it's a feeling of contentedness, of having just the right amount of things, the right amount of time.

The Swedes happen to have a word for exactly that: *lagom*. The modern meaning roughly translates to "just right." Not too much, not too little . . . just something in the middle, the moderate choice between two extremes. Lagom is a thread that ties many parts of Swedish society and culture together, the cornerstone of personal behavior, design ethos, and community. There is no quantifiable amount of lagom, which can sometimes make it hard to grasp exactly what it is. Lagom is part personal balance and part social understanding, something that's good for us and the world around us. As we strive to manage our busy everyday lives, lagom might just be the key that we need to unlock a more intentional, balanced, healthy lifestyle.

As the daughter of a Swedish expat, I grew up not loving lagom. Certainly, it was a word commonly used in my household: "How much food do you want?" "Lagom." "How much coffee should I pour?" "Lagom," but as a driver of behavior, lagom was to be avoided. My mother, an artist, was born and raised in Sweden. For her, lagom represented the structure of the restrictive Swedish social box that she had wanted to leave in her twenties, moving to the American West Coast where social expectations were at a bare minimum and she felt that she had more freedom to be who she wanted to be. In my mother's view, lagom was less about balance and more about the social equalizer; the thing that restrained you, kept you from being able to fully express who you were and what you wanted.

But as I have grown older and started to think about lagom in more complex ways, I see how it trickled into our family life regardless, perhaps in ways that weren't immediately apparent to my mother or myself. While our

family was eccentric in its own ways, we were lagom as well, channeling a Swedish approach to the world around us. We always ate balanced meals, full of whole grains and vegetables, and we tried to reduce our impact on the environment as best we could, my mother tending the compost in the garden and washing out plastic bags to be reused. I grew up with the mantra that good things cost money, that when you buy quality, you are making a long-term investment, not one dictated by trends or fleeting interests. My parents believed in the value of public school, that social good came from the benefit of an entire community, not just an individual. Our sofas were covered in wool blankets and our cupboards full of textiles made from natural fibers. Perhaps our lifestyle wasn't so lagom vis-à-vis our American neighbors (who most likely thought that we were a bit extreme in our ways), but it certainly was representative of a more Swedish approach to living, one that was moderate and mindful.

HOW LAGOM CAN BALANCE OUR MODERN WORLD

In today's modern Western world, we function with a "go big or go home" mentality. We strive to be the very best version of ourselves, the version that looks good to the outside world. That makes for fast-paced lives. We're overworked and overbooked. We go from one task to another, juggling to-do lists and pushing through exhaustion. We flip through glossy lifestyle magazines full of images of what we wish our lives looked like, comparing ourselves and our homes to staged versions of reality. We see our friends and their glorious lives showcased on social media.

Our expectations of what we can do, and what we should do, are far beyond anything we're able to realistically achieve. We show one side of ourselves publicly: the glossy, put-together, happy-no-matter-what side, and keep the other locked away in private. More and more of us are stressed, strained, and burnt out.

This all comes at a social cost, not to mention an environmental one. We are more and more afraid of our neighbors; hate and fear guide how we view the world instead of compassion and community. We live larger and larger—our houses, our cars, our appetites—our overall impact on the Earth ever increasing. As we start to meet our own personal limits, and society and the environment meet theirs, many of us are asking ourselves what changes we can make. How can we live better?

There is no easy pill for a healthy, sustainable, balanced lifestyle, one that will change your life overnight, but a lagom approach may be part of the answer. For me, when I think about lagom, it isn't about behaving in an average, acceptable way, or holding back. Instead, it is about finding balance in my everyday life. It is about focusing on the common good as opposed to the individual—the idea that when society thrives, so do we as people, which is a philosophy that extends from our workplaces to the environment.

Applying a sense of lagom to our everyday lives—be it in what we eat, what we wear, how we live, how we work—might just be the trick for embracing a more balanced, sustainable lifestyle that welcomes the pleasures of existence rather than those of consumption; the antidote to our modern, consumptive world. Lagom is, after all, based on the principles of simplicity and moderation. In a world of lagom, less is more.

Too much of a good thing and it's hard to see the good any longer. Think of having a slice of decadent cake, and how indulgent it feels. Think about what it feels like to have a second; no matter how hard you try, it's rarely better than the first one. That same principle can apply to all avenues of our lives. If we spent our lives on holiday, it would be hard to find the joy in holidays. Indulgence feels good because we *don't* have it all the time. We want to strive after the balance that keeps us on an even keel.

This book is an introduction to lagom; what it is and how you might apply it to various aspects of your daily life. This is not in order to be more Swedish, but to be more balanced and fulfilled, to get out of the rat race of our modern-day society and take time to be mindfully in the present. It is a book that embraces slow living.

LAGOM

adverb
just right; *nog* just enough; *tillräckligt* sufficiently;
måttligt in moderation, moderately

adjektiv
tillräcklig adequate, sufficient; *lämplig el. passande*
fitting, appropriate, suitable; *måttlig* moderate

NORDSTEDTS ORDBOK

THE MEANING OF LAGOM

Lagom, phonetically written "lɑːˌgɔm" and for the English
speaker pronounced "lah-gom," is a Swedish word with
old roots.

If you ask Swedes about the history of lagom, many
might begin with a story of Vikings. It's a romanticized
version of lagom's roots, a story of the Vikings passing
around a horn of mead. *Laget om,* or "around the team,"
meant that the mead had to make it to everyone's lips,
requiring that each Viking only take an adequate sip

so that there would be some for everyone. Told many times over, this explanation is a popular folk etymology, a mistaken account of lagom's roots.

The roots are a little more basic than that and, in fact, quite telling as to why lagom as a concept functions the way it does in modern Swedish culture. In Swedish, *lag* means "law" and in Old Swedish, "laguhm" translates roughly as "according to the law." In other words, proper and suitable behavior within a society. In this sense, lagom is a social construct that relates to creating a just society, encouraging members of society to not just abide by the written law, but also to practice common sense.

Today, that original meaning has modernized and shifted slightly, but it still carries the same social impact. Lagom is often translated into English as "not too much, not too little, just right." It's a word that implies an understanding of what the extremes are, and finding the more moderate path in between the two. It means behaving appropriately, eating the right amount and, on the flip side, celebrating the right amount too.

In Swedish it's an all-encompassing word, one that can be applied to almost every element of society. Lagom food, lagom drink, lagom work hours; the idea that

a balanced amount of everything leads to a just and equal society and, overall, a good life. You can also use the word to imply that something wasn't so good. To say that a meal was *lagom bra*, "lagom good," means that, in fact, it was not so great. If something is *lagom roligt*, "lagom fun," then no, it was not so fun at all.

CAN ONLY THE SWEDES LIVE LAGOM?

To Swedes, lagom is an ingrained part of their culture. It is such a normal concept that it's not one that Swedes regularly give a lot of thought to. It just *is*. "How would you write a whole book about lagom?" my 102-year-old grandmother asked my mother when she told her that I was working on this book. I think I could classify my *mormor* as the "queen of lagom"; a woman who cuts the thinnest slices of our family Christmas fruitcake, but also liberally spreads butter on sandwiches and in her later years took to drinking a glass of wine with dinner because her doctor told her it might be good for her. She is not a woman of excess, but she is a woman who knows how to find enjoyment in the smallest things. Until the age of one hundred, she would go on walks to pick wildflowers and branches to place on the kitchen table. Her coffee breaks have always been paired with a baked good. Maybe her embodiment of lagom, her enjoyment in moderation and simplicity, has been a part of her secret for such a long life.

After I asked my good Swedish friend Kerstin about her perceptions of lagom, she brought it up with her colleagues at work. She mentioned that being forced to

think about it led to an interesting conversation between all of them. "*Precis som man vill ha det*," said one of them, meaning, "Just like you want things to be."

I like this understanding of lagom, the idea that it's about having just the right amount in your life that you feel content. This is not to say that there is never excess in Sweden. Some may point to the drinking culture, or the abundance of food come Christmas time. Certainly, there are moments in Swedish culture that veer from the norm but, overall, Sweden is a country where moderation finds its way into individual behavior, fashion, food, and beyond. As the rest of us find ourselves swinging from one extreme to another, bingeing on treats one moment and detoxing the next, this idea of lagom can start to sound appealing, a way to enjoy a little bit of everything.

The Swedish proverb *lagom är bäst* says that "lagom is best." In other words, everything in moderation. How many treats should you indulge in? Lagom är bäst. How many overtime hours should you put in at work? Lagom är bäst. Whatever you are doing in your life, don't overdo it, just do the right amount. There's even an emphasized version of the word, *precis lagom*, the idea that something is perfectly lagom—absolutely just right.

Lagom, as a word and as a social concept, is so integrated into Swedish culture that Sweden is sometimes referred to as *landet lagom*, "the land of lagom." Outside of Sweden we've been making this association for a long time, often influenced by the Swedish political model, which has led to Sweden being viewed as the land that finds its success not in the extremes, but somewhere in the middle.

This has led many to believe that the word lagom only exists in Swedish, and that somehow the concept is inherently Swedish, one that only Swedes can understand and identify with. It's easy to make assumptions about people based on their language, but let us take a moment to dive into the world of linguistics, which teaches us that just because a language has a specific word, does not mean that the behavior indicated by that word is particular to that one culture.

Take the Danish word *hygge*, for example, a long-standing concept within Denmark but one which took the world by storm in 2016. The word may not have a direct translation in other languages, but the Danes certainly aren't alone in creating cozy moments. "People do *hygge* in other countries even if they don't have a word for it," says Mikael Parkvall, author of *Lagom finns bara i Sverige och andra myter om språk* (*Lagom is Only Swedish and Other Myths About Language*) and lecturer at Stockholm University's Department of Linguistics.

Lagom is exactly the same. "It's possible that Swedes are more lagom [in their nature], but we should be careful to draw a connection between the language and the people," says Parkvall. "Other people in the world might think that things should be lagom, they just don't have a specific word for it."

What he means is that we don't have to be Swedish to understand, or even embrace, the concept of lagom. "There is no one in the world who doesn't understand that there is something in between too little and too much," says Parkvall. In fact this concept of moderation, and living in a just and balanced way, is not reserved for Sweden; it is far more global. Ancient Greek had *pan metron ariston*, "everything in moderation." According to Parkvall, in more modern languages, Estonian has *paras* and Finnish has *sopiva*, which both come with a similar meaning to lagom. In English we have the proverbial "all good things in moderation." Balance and moderation extend across cultures; most of us know that we could probably use a little more of them.

It is easy to generalize that Sweden is perhaps more "lagom" in nature than other countries. Particularly having grown up in the United States, I can quickly make the gross generalization that Swedish culture is lagom and American culture is quite the opposite. In the eye of the outside world, Sweden has a reputation for existing somewhere in between the extremes—cool, calm, and collected. There are always exceptions, but many of us are charmed by Sweden because overall the country and its people have seemed to find a balance that leaves them healthy, happy, and successful. Even when its policies are progressive—and they often are—those policies feel in tune and in balance with what should be.

For Swedes, that lagom reputation "can be both positive and negative," says Parkvall. You're just as likely to hear someone's satisfaction with the idea of lagom as someone saying, "We Swedes, why do we have to be so lagom all the time?" says Parkvall. Not every Swede loves lagom. Some see it as the guiding principle, and others see it as restrictive, something that keeps them from excelling, stifles them and limits them from pushing boundaries. "It's not like the word represents a national religion in Sweden," says Parkvall.

IS THERE A DARKER SIDE TO LAGOM?

We can't look at lagom without looking at the Swedish political and social structure. Here, where environmental policies are innovative and more than half of energy comes from renewables, parents get over a year of paid leave days per child, life expectancy is just over eighty years, and the country finds itself among the ten happiest in the world, life is good. By all accounts, the Swedish model has provided a social and economic structure where the majority thrives.

The consideration for the wellbeing of the group as opposed to just the individual is a guiding principle of Swedish politics and culture, the idea that everyone should have access to the same rights and benefits. It is these socio and political underpinnings that are at the core of lagom. What's moderate is good for us all. When everyone is treated as an equal, society thrives, and part of lagom is taking part in communal society: you don't take too little or too much.

Of course, this mindset veers close to the much more negatively viewed *Jantelagen*, "The Law of Jante." This outline of social norms comes from Aksel Sandemosse's book *En flyktning krysser sitt spor* (*A Fugitive Crosses His Tracks*), first published in Denmark in 1933. In it, Sandemose describes a fictional town of Jante and the ten laws that dictate the social behavior of its residents.

The ten rules create a structure where everyone is equal, an attitude that you'll find across the Scandinavian countries, which from the outset sounds nice but, broken down, leads to many cultural issues. Lagom and Jante Law "have a common ancestor in terms of rural society's equalizing effect, keeping things balanced and sharing out the resources, a tendency which was amplified by Lutheranism," says Michael Booth, author of *The Almost Nearly Perfect People: The Myth of the Scandinavian Utopia*. The major downfall of Jante Law is that "We are all equal," quickly becomes "Don't stand out from your neighbor," "Don't believe that you are someone special," and today the term describes the act of discouraging individuality, overachievement, and anything that stands out from the cultural norm—the Scandinavian version of social conformity. While it has changed over the decades, these are cultural mores that many who move to Sweden, and the rest of Scandinavia, can often struggle with, particularly if they come from more outgoing cultures

where individualism is celebrated. Jante Law "encourages a general disapproval of ambition, or of competitiveness, which I think affects kids the most: smart, high achievers are still often squashed at school, particularly if they are academic high achievers," says Booth. "It's fine to be good at handball or team sports, as long as you don't make a big thing out of it."

Sweden is not alone in this overall attitude. Australia deals with its own Tall Poppy Syndrome, also felt in other English-speaking countries like New Zealand and Canada. There's a Dutch proverb that's similar too: *hoge bomen vangen veel wind* or "tall trees catch a lot of wind." These are all social constraints that on the one hand can help to ensure that everyone is treated equally, but on the other hand can easily restrain people instead of challenging them, teaching them that they shouldn't stand out or, even worse, lead to cutting down anyone who succeeds or stands out from the crowd.

THE BENEFITS OF LIVING LAGOM

As with all things in life, the perfect balance is to be found in the middle, and there are many lessons that we can learn from the Swedish concept of lagom and apply to our own lives.

Lagom allows us to remove ourselves from the extremes, to find balance in the middle. Extremes can often be detrimental to our physical and emotional health. We overeat and overindulge, then find ourselves trying to stick to a strictly defined regime of food to compensate. As soon as we're finished, we're back to overindulging. At the office, we put in long, stressed hours, never happy with our work, constantly striving to be "the best." We bring our work home with us, checking our email in between making dinner and putting the kids to bed. We are left distracted, exhausted, and feeling far from successful. We feel like we don't have any control over our lives as we're attempting to do too many things, but do none of them well.

Our modern lifestyles have become driven by the principles of taking as much as we can, doing as much as we can, pushing as hard as we can, and overextending ourselves far past our personal limits and those of the environment. These excessive lifestyles come at a cost. We're unhealthy physically and mentally, as is the world around us. Perhaps the idea of lagom has something to offer us.

There is no easy answer to all of these things, no pill that we can take to quickly solve our modern-day stresses and problems, but what we must learn from the idea of lagom is that we allow ourselves to be "just enough." We can work to find happiness in who we are, not who we plan to be.

In today's modern culture of fashion and design magazines, celebrities, and social media, we're constantly inundated with what we think we "should" be. "I should work out more. I should socialize more. I should get more sleep. I should eat better. I should have a better job. I should cook more. I should learn a new language. I should be traveling. I should learn how to [insert new activity here]."

Instead of using these impulses to challenge us to develop as human beings, they become obstacles, and instead of inspiration, reasons to berate ourselves. They hinder instead of provide encouragement. They drive us toward a social competition that leaves us exhausted.

We aren't satisfied with what we have and who we are. We are instead constantly on the pursuit for more. "If only I can get to the next step, then I'll be happy." This personal and social rat race becomes difficult to escape, and once on this track we're only focused on that next step, which we think will lead to happiness, peace, and contentment. But these are things that can only be found in the present, in that space where we are living in balance with ourselves and the world around us.

It would be incorrect to assume that lagom means holding back, that if we are able to find satisfaction with who we are and where we are in life we will become static. As humans, we are always learning, always developing. Lagom does not mean putting all of that on hold, but it means finding happiness in our own evolution as individuals, wherever that evolution leads. If we don't end up becoming renowned within our field, or if we don't end up making a six-figure salary, that is OK. Who we are is not defined by our successes or our failures, we are defined by how we live with them.

Lagom's benefits are not limited to personal ones. In this modern world where we live large, our footprint has taken a toll. We have bigger houses and bigger cars.

We buy more and, in turn, throw away more. We live lives of excess and waste. When we are more moderate about our choices, we reduce our impact. Applying elements of lagom to our everyday lives can not only make us feel better, but also help us to pursue a more sustainable path, because when we are satisfied with just the right amount of all things, we live in better balance with ourselves, our community, and our environment.

Live Lagom is a challenge for you to think about slow living. In the same way that the Slow Food movement has brought more awareness to what we eat, where it comes from, and how we prepare it, a slow life is an intentional life, one that doesn't take too much or cause any harm, and one that focuses on the essential.

This book is broken up into four main categories: work, home, health, and environment. In all of them we look at ways to live more lagom, to be more intentional and mindful, to live better with less.

LAGOM AT WORK

Striving for work–life balance is not just an individual pursuit in Sweden, but a national one.

According to the OECD, in 2016 the average Swedish worker clocked around 1,600 hours in the year. To put that number in perspective, the average in the UK was 1,700 and 1,800 in the United States. Only about 1 percent of Swedish workers work long hours, one of the lowest rates among the OECD countries, where the average is 13 percent, limiting the negative effects for Swedes often associated with long work hours, such as personal health and stress. Understanding the social value of fewer working hours, there was a recent two-year government initiative in Sweden to test a six-hour work day. For example, nurses at a retirement community in Gothenburg kept their pay levels but decreased their work hours. The result was socially positive—nurses felt healthier, had reduced sick leave and patient care improved. But the experiment came at a significant economic cost, resulting from having to hire more help to cover the time that the nurses weren't at work. In the short term, that means that everyone won't be switching over to a shorter work week; however, the study did highlight the social impact of reduced time at work, pointing out that this could certainly be a part of a long-term solution and a consideration for policymakers.

Sweden is a country of many work benefits, from paid parent leave to sabbaticals to extensive paid holiday, all policies that create a social structure focused on the wellbeing of all its citizens. Parents, for example, who have to stay home from work when a child is sick, have access to a government smartphone app that they can use to file for their benefits, which allows them to be paid for their child's sick day. The minimum amount of paid holiday days in Sweden is twenty-five, although many workers enjoy more.

This is all to say that work culture in Sweden is as much on account of the cultural perception of and attitude towards work as the policies structured around it. In a sense, when it comes to work–life balance, the Swedish government has taken the lagom approach—not too much, not too little, just right—and the population is better off for it.

If we don't live in Sweden, while we can't do a lot in the short term to change our own country's policies that affect work–life balance, we can change our own attitude towards work, cultivating an approach that's focused around the concepts of lagom.

FINDING OUR OWN WORK-LIFE BALANCE

Unless we're inordinately rich and can spend our days doing whatever we please, we must make money to put food on the table and a roof over our heads. For most of us, there is no getting around the fact that we have to work. It's also important to remember that contemplating work–life balance is, in many ways, a luxury. If we have the space to think about how we want to find a better balance between work and our personal lives, it implies that we have the means to live and aren't worried about where the next paycheck is coming from. Being able to consider how to better our work–life balance is something that deserves our gratitude.

We have a tendency to approach work–life balance by starting with the question "How can I work less?" What if we instead asked ourselves "How can I work better?"

Working better means working more efficiently, more productively, more creatively, more collaboratively. Quality work doesn't necessarily mean working more hours, just as working fewer hours doesn't always mean producing work of lesser quality. In fact, working better can help us to do the same work in less time, in turn providing an answer to that first question. To find the balance, we have to learn to be smarter about how we work: planning, prioritizing, and setting our own limits so that we are successful in the work that we do.

THE IMPORTANCE OF BREAKS

If we've ever had to hunker down and finish something no matter what, we know how difficult that can be. We all find ourselves procrastinating and tidying our desks rather than just getting on with it. Instead, we should make time for a real break, with many studies showing the importance of breaks in improving productivity.

A social custom that Swedish business leaders often point to as a reason for efficiency, productivity, and the general wellbeing of their workers is *fika*, the Swedish coffee break. A common custom at Swedish workplaces, a fika break usually occurs in the mid-morning and early afternoon. It is the chance to grab a cup of coffee, step away from the computer, and sit down for a chat with co-workers. Sometimes a co-worker might bring in a few Swedish baked goods to share. This is such a common custom that workplaces often refer to the break room as the *fikarum,* "the fika room." While coffee is traditionally the focal point of fika, the purpose is not just a caffeinated pick-me-up. Instead, it's a moment to take a step away from work, socialize, and be present while not focusing on deadlines or other work-induced stress.

Even if you're not in a workplace with colleagues, take a fika break on your own. A ten- or fifteen-minute break away from the computer while you drink your cup of coffee or mug of tea will do you a world of good, leaving you refreshed and renewed to come back to the task at hand.

QUALITY OVER QUANTITY

In the workplace, a key concept of lagom is focusing on doing what's needed and doing it well, rather than accomplishing a bunch of superfluous tasks to simply look busy. In the workplace, Swedes are known for focusing on the essential. That means prioritizing tasks and analyzing what work really needs to be done, both elements of working smarter.

As an American, I'm used to the attitude that honors long work hours. Putting in an extensive week at the office can be seen as a sign of importance and a commitment to getting a job done. Tell someone that you just did the right amount of work to get the job done and that person might raise his or her eyebrows, wondering why you lack ambition. But in Sweden, where there is a more balanced approach to work and life, working longer hours can be seen as the sign of inefficiency; that you weren't able to do the job well to begin with, and you were therefore forced to stay longer.

Doing a lagom amount of work to get the job done well can obviously be hard to gauge, but if we retrain ourselves to think more about the quality of the work

and less about the quantity of the work, we can find that balance. That also means focusing on being efficient, identifying what's a priority and what isn't. It means distancing ourselves from so-called "busy work." It means perhaps one less hour in the morning casually perusing emails and chatting with a co-worker to ease into the day and, instead, an hour of focused work to complete a task.

There are a few other action items that fit into this category of quality over quantity:

Reduce multitasking

Taking on too many tasks not only throws off our balance, but it can lead to being less productive. Sending emails while on a call, switching quickly back and forth between projects, finishing a report while researching the next one. While we may have the illusion of getting many things done at once, multitasking has been shown to significantly decrease our productivity.

Instead, we should create time to focus on a single task or project. This can be difficult for a lot of us, especially those who are used to multitasking. Start small. Turn your phone on silent, close your email and your Internet browser, and focus on nothing but the task at hand for an hour. Close your office door. Don't take calls. While your brain will at first crave a distraction, as you get more and more used to spending time on focused tasks, you'll be able to do it for longer.

Thinking vs. action

Have you ever heard of the term "analysis paralysis"? It's a term often used for overthinking a decision, but it can also be applied to work tasks. Spending too much time overthinking a project can lead to that feeling of being so entirely overwhelmed that instead of tackling the project, we avoid it entirely. The next time you're feeling stuck, spend more time doing and less time thinking. In other words, a lagom amount of thinking and planning, and a lagom amount of action.

Planning and prioritizing

An essential part of having a balanced workload is spreading it out over time, and this requires planning. You want to work proactively not reactively, and without planning and prioritizing tasks, it's easy to feel overloaded and overwhelmed as you never feel that you're able to get on top of your workload. Some weeks may require work that goes above and beyond the normal level, but if for the most part your workload is balanced, you'll feel better about the occasional time spent doing a little extra.

CULTIVATING A CULTURE OF COLLABORATION AND COMMUNITY

As we discussed in the introduction, Swedish culture is very much about the benefit of the society as a whole as opposed to just the success of the individual, and this plays out in the business world as well. In their book *The Seven Cultures of Capitalism*, Charles Hampden-Turner and Alfons Trompenaars point out that finding lagom in the workplace is discovering that "somewhere in between the opinions expressed lies an optimal position." In other words, consensus. Workers from other, more individual-focused cultures can struggle with this in the business environment. Decisions can take longer because they require everyone's input, working hard to find the lagom point, or the middle ground.

A collaborative workplace is one built on trust and understanding. It's a safe space where a worker can bring up tough issues and questions without the fear of being fired or reprimanded. You can do this among your own colleagues, encouraging them to speak up and talk through things together.

When input from all sides is valued, the entire team is invested. Honoring collaboration creates a workspace where not one individual carries the load of responsibility, and this in turn is helpful in reducing stress. If you're working on a project with colleagues, be aware of the shared workload, so that it is evenly split between everyone.

Cultivating a culture of collaboration also helps us come up with even better ideas than we can on our own. Collaborating is good for a creative spark; we are challenged to think differently about things, making our brains connect the dots in new ways. Working outside of just ourselves means the chance for new ideas and new approaches.

When we focus solely on individualism, we focus on what we need to succeed, which keeps us from thinking about what those around us need to succeed. If we are satisfied with the success of the group, then we are less apt to be pursuing individual success at all costs, which can easily lead to boasting and the kind of ego-driven behavior that quickly becomes off-putting. Talking about the crazy seventy-hour week we just did and how it led to a great success is the opposite of lagom. In a more collaborative work culture, it matters less who takes responsibility for the success of a project because the quality of the work comes from a place of collaboration. Instead of shouting to your office mates about how much you've done for a project, let your work speak for itself, and honor the work of those around you.

A longstanding critique of this lagom approach to the workplace is that it doesn't always provide the right incentive for people to feel that they should aspire to do more. In a lagom culture, you're not always rewarded for being the best and the brightest, and a drawback to lagom is that it can stifle thought leaders and anyone striving to do business out of the box. This can leave workers feeling as if they are stagnating, and can also make it harder for people with an entrepreneurial spirit. It's a reason I have heard from many Swedish expats for moving to a culture that was more encouraging for people who wanted to push beyond the norm, and which allowed them to achieve their full potential.

But that too is changing. Sweden has started to make a name for itself as a conducive place for start-ups, with cities like Gothenburg and Stockholm cultivating the kind of place that is attractive to potential entrepreneurs, like accelerators, incubators, co-working spaces, etc.

Sweden has become a European tech hub, with leading tech companies such as Skype and Spotify based in Stockholm. Today's younger generation of Swedes has either traveled or worked abroad, and speaks impeccable English. Being a small country in terms of size and population, shifting to a global focus can expand Swedish business opportunities. This has all made for an opening to the outside world, which in turn has helped to globalize the focus of many Swedish companies. They have found that happy middle ground of just enough of Swedish business culture and just enough of that of the outside world to find the so-called lagom business model that works well.

ALLOWING OURSELVES TO BE "GOOD ENOUGH"

At work, our managers and our co-workers judge our performance but, more importantly, we also judge ourselves. You don't have to look that far to realize that in today's modern culture messages about what we should be striving for and what we should achieve strike us from every direction. We are told that we can have it all, sold a vision of perfection that is in reality, unachievable.

Instead of perfection, a lagom lifestyle is about finding balance in being "good enough," where we can allow ourselves to enjoy satisfaction in a job well done that is performed within appropriate boundaries. We may not rise to the status of CEO or a six-figure salary, but if these are things that we want—or what we think we want—then we have to ask ourselves if we can live with the costs they come with.

Every job comes at a price, every job requires compromise. Pursuing a career as a creative freelancer might mean a lower salary but has the perk of a flexible schedule. A traditional nine-to-five job may have less flexibility but more monetary stability. Ultimately, these choices are our own to make, and they require us to focus on what is important to us, and which elements we see as essential and which ones we are willing to let go of. Being good enough is not about being the best, it is about identifying what our strengths and desires are and then allowing ourselves to be satisfied with the outcome, even if the outcome doesn't look like the life that we are sold in a magazine or in an advertisement.

To have it all is a myth. But to have what we want in a reasonable amount can be achievable if we let go of our expectations and self-judgments. We have to stop comparing ourselves to others.

A close Swedish friend of mine with two small children often says to me, "I don't know how other people do it." By "do it" she means have a family, maintain a career and a household, and still have personal time. While Sweden has a culture of lagom, that culture has also grown to include modern expectations of what success means—big salary, big house—and they take a toll, resulting in sick leave on account of burn out and high stress levels.

We all know that feeling of stress, and of feeling like we're only barely managing to keep things together.

The secret is that while it may look like other people are managing perfectly fine, often they are not. They too are stressed. Marriages suffer, families suffer, all from attempting to maintain a lifestyle deemed successful by cultural standards.

These standards can also inhibit our work. Dreaming big and having ambition is often an important part of pushing us towards something new. But it can also be inhibiting. The pressure to do something amazing and unique can paralyze us. We should dream big, we should aim high, but we have to also understand that sometimes those aspirations can stop us in our tracks. Often, it's only in setting aside our ambitions, in allowing ourselves to be "good enough," that we are able to do the work that needs to be done.

There's no one answer to these problems of socially induced stress, but finding a better satisfaction in who we are and where we are in the present, not who we dream of being or where we dream of being in the future, is one path to bringing more balance, and happiness, into our everyday. We are social creatures, but technology has helped to exacerbate all of that socially induced stress.

Taking breaks from social media, or even removing ourselves for large chunks of time, can help us to focus inward on what matters instead of focusing outward and constantly comparing ourselves to others. That's not always an easy task; jumping off the social hamster wheel takes commitment and work. But if we are able to identify what our true goals are—ones that we define, not the ones that society defines—then we are better equipped to lead a life that is successful on our own terms.

Remember: You. Are. Enough.

KNOWING WHEN TO TAKE A HOLIDAY

The definition of a successful Swedish lifestyle is not
necessarily one that's filled with overtime. Instead it's
one where you feel good about the work that you do, but
this work is also balanced with time away from it. With a
healthy number of paid holidays, this is easy for Swedes to
accomplish, but even if we have paid holidays allotted
to us, unless we have an attitude that embraces the idea
of work–life balance, it can be easy to squander those
days away. And in some cases, not take them at all. If we
have put work on a pedestal above all else, then we don't
allow ourselves the very necessary and beneficial time
away from work, and if we don't, we can easily suffer
both physically and mentally. We have to train ourselves
to find the balance of a lagom amount of work and
a lagom amount of play.

   That's hard for a lot of us (sometimes even Swedes).
Today, we live in an ever-growing culture of "busy."
We fill our days to the brim, be it with work or social
engagements. We can't see a friend because we're too busy.
We can't go for a walk because we're too busy. We haven't
been able to finish reading a book because we're too busy.

When we're asked, "How have you been?" our default response is often, "Oh I am *so* busy these days." In modern Western culture, being busy has come to define us—the socially acceptable pastime. It comes with an underlying assumption that if we're busy, with our schedules packed to the brim, then we must be important, our lives must have meaning and purpose. We use busy as a plaster to cover up the real question that we're all afraid of asking: if we are not busy, then who are we?

The truth is that we're too busy being busy to take a step back and ask ourselves: what exactly are we busy with? Sometimes we've got a work schedule full of deadlines and it's hard to get around that. But more often than not, we're filling up our time off with a multitude of activities instead of taking the time to just exist.

Swedes counter their focus on work with a value on relaxation that we could all learn from. A few weeks of summer vacation might be spent at a rural cottage, away from the demands of modern life and with the opportunity to slow down and be in the present. This is time well spent, as it's truly rejuvenating, leaving the person ready to tackle work and the routine of everyday life when he or she returns.

But you don't have to escape to the countryside to find that kind of calmness. The goal is to allow ourselves—be at ease with—days where we do "nothing." If our schedules are always packed full, we don't have time for reflection or rest. In fact, "doing nothing" is a bit of a misnomer. When we allow ourselves time to slow down and be in the present, we are actually doing a lot for our general health and wellbeing. We need time that isn't scheduled, we need time where we have the luxury of moving from a cup of coffee to a book and back again. We need slow moments.

We have a tendency to think of slow moments as boring moments. If we're not occupied with something then what are we accomplishing? But these slow moments are essential to our health, and even our creativity. The brain needs space to daydream.

These types of breaks don't only have to come during vacations; we can make time for them throughout the year. Make time for small vacations and excursions, even day trips. Perhaps it's a weekend in another city, perhaps it's a day at home when you don't look at the to-do list and you let your mind just wander. You have to find what works for you, but achieving work–life balance is as much about

thinking what you do with your work hours as thinking about what you do with your off hours. A lagom lifestyle is one that's intentional on both ends; one that leaves time for being still and in the present in between the moments of chaos.

This also means that we have to get better at time "unplugged." Digital devices have made it so that we rarely take time that's truly "off." Instead, we are constantly on and connected, responding to an email, messaging a friend, scrolling through a newsfeed. These activities quickly fill our time. Think how easy it is to look at Facebook, and all of a sudden half an hour has gone by. Or how easy it is to come home after a long day at work and watch an episode of a television series. That episode quickly turns to another one, and then another one. Suddenly several hours have passed.

What could we have done with that time instead? Sometimes we need to indulge in these activities, but I am certain that the majority of us spend far more time doing them than we should—definitely not a lagom amount.

Finding work–life balance is about prioritizing, making room for the things that we decide are essential. "I don't have the time," is often a replacement for "I don't take the time." There are a limited amount of hours in the day—time is precious—what we do with them is entirely up to us. We won't ever get more time, we have to learn to take it. Our happiness and balance is in our own hands.

LAGOM AT HOME

That whatever is useful is worthy of respect, all women realize; that whatever is beautiful is worthy of being loved, many realize; but that the only thing worth striving for is harmony between the useful and the beautiful—how many realize that?

ELLEN KEY

DESIGN AND ARCHITECTURE

Functional design is the backbone of Swedish society, a reflection of physical and cultural identity.

Swedish design is borne out of the environment, both in style and materials. Light is essential in the winter and revered in the summer, a central element to Swedish buildings and interiors and a reason for the strength of the Swedish glass industry. The forests have long provided timber, the ground gives birth to fibers like linen and wool and, farther below, bears iron and steel. Swedish design is a reflection of place.

Design and architecture are inextricably linked to the social and cultural influences of the places they are from, making these reflections of place both physical (within the materials used) and cultural (what the designs stand for). Current Swedish design has its roots in the early twentieth century, a time that gave rise to the modernist movement. The focus was on form and function, something that's still a cornerstone of Swedish design. The design of the era was borne out of theidea that good design can improve lives. *Vackrare vardagsvara (Better Things for Everyday Life)* was the title of Gregor Paulsson's influential text published in 1919. This movement also posited a belief that style is not reserved for the elite few, that good design should be available for everyone.

These principles gave rise to Scandinavian modern design, gaining international notoriety in the 1950s and 1960s and, along with it, many of the iconic designs and Scandinavian design names that we still recognize today: Arne Jacobsen, Stig Lindberg, Alvar Aalto, Poul Henningsen, Jørn Utzon, Gunnar Asplund, and Greta Grossman.

Today, this style of design is still very popular globally, well recognized and implemented by interior designers around the world. This is the period of design—and the period that continued to inspire Swedish design for decades—that we often think of when we hear the words "Swedish design." Because of it, we have a tendency to think of Swedish design as very clean and minimal. However, there are other styles that are just as integral to Swedish design culture. Look no further than Josef Frank. The Austrian-born designer was a leader in Swedish textile and furniture design, creating bold and intricate patterns that are still well known and can be found in many Swedish homes today. The Finnish design house Marimekko and the former Swedish collective Ten Swedish Designers (10-Gruppen) provide yet more examples of bold Scandinavian patterns.

But even within wild colors and patterns, there is always a certain Swedish sensibility, never feeling overdone or outlandish. Ultimately, Swedish design always brings a balanced approach, for a look that is simultaneously bright and vibrant while still feeling clean and simple. "Pattern is calming," wrote

Josef Frank, whose work, while intricate, colorful and wild, has a meditative element to it, just like many other Swedish textile designers. Vibrant patterns have come to define Swedish textiles and, paired with more neutral, minimalist elements, can help to balance a space.

DESIGN IN THE SWEDISH HOME

One of the most important elements of design in Sweden is that it's not reserved for the elite few—design makes an appearance in the everyday. It is intertwined with the social values discussed in the introduction. The book *Swedish Design: An Ethnography* by Keith Murphy takes a close look at the intersection of cultural norms and design. In Sweden, "Design becomes a tool for improving individual practices, common problems, and shared needs. It is not treated as a specialty service or an obstacle to profit, but rather the basic starting point for crafting a just society. In Sweden, so the cultural model goes, design is everywhere and belongs to everyone."

This is perhaps why we are so taken with Swedish design in the outside world. In other places, design is considered something for those with means; a well-designed house or a piece of art on the wall only attainable with a certain paycheck. "Good taste" is inextricably linked to class. But when we look at Sweden, it seems that every element of life looks good, down to the very simplest of objects. Something as mundane as a newspaper laid out next to a tea mug on a kitchen table is turned into something special. The right amount of design and beauty appears in everyday objects.

A large part of this is because of the Swedish cultural focus on the home, the primary site where design touches the surface of everyday experience at the smallest level of detail. This importance dates back to the national romantic movement of the late nineteenth and early twentieth centuries. The most well known of Swedish figures in this movement was Carl Larsson, a painter and author whose iconic works can be found throughout Swedish culture today, from postcards to sandwich trays. He made the home the focal point, honing in on the intimate spaces and routines of everyday life. While she didn't receive as much attention as her husband, Carl's wife, Karin Larsson, was also an artist and largely responsible for much of this focus. Many of the elements in Larsson's paintings are still basic elements of Swedish home design today—kitchen benches, potted plants, wooden floors covered in rag rugs, the muted tones of greys and blues that Swedish homes are known for.

Feminist and social critic Ellen Key also tackled the subject of home, but in a more direct way. In her 1889 collection of essays *Skönhet för Alla* (*Beauty for Everyone*), inspired by William Morris and the Arts and Crafts movement, she advocated for the power of beauty, explaining how to make the beautiful accessible not to just an elite few, but to everyone. This laid the groundwork for designers and artists to bring beauty into even mass-produced products. Her argument was that an object serves a purpose—like a table for eating—but that it should also fulfill this purpose with "simplicity and ease, with delicacy and expressivity." An object should not be beautiful at the cost of functionality, or vice versa. The ideal is found in the balance in between.

Today, the home is where we see the concept of lagom play out visually, a space of balance that embodies the cultural values of Swedish society. It is still where beauty finds an entry point to the everyday. This is what makes Swedish interiors feel special: the balance between how they look and how they function.

A lagom approach to style has made Swedish designs classic and timeless, which has resulted in the balanced feeling that emanates from Swedish interiors. "Neither the designer or the consumer wants to stick out, but on the other hand, doesn't want to disappear amongst the

masses," says Frida Ramstedt, founder of Scandinavia's leading interior blog, *Trendenser*. "The result is design with moderation and perfection, but also with a long life, since the design takes up a lagom amount of space, are lagom trendy and require lagom energy intensive."

Not Just a House, a Home

As humans, we desire to create a home, to "nest," so to say. Since the beginning of time we have been building spaces to take shelter in. We want that home space to be safe, to protect us from the outside world. Today, a home provides us with a physical and an emotional shelter.

Creating a space that you love means creating a home, and not just a house. This allows for a sense of balance within your home space, one that encourages you to be content in the now. When we live in a space that we love, one that is in balance with our personality and needs, we are also less likely to constantly be searching for more "things" to make it better; we are content with what we have.

With the "not too much, not too little, just right" definition of lagom, it's easy to jump to the conclusion that a lagom-designed home is a minimal home. The appeal of Scandinavian minimalism is at an all-time high—just pick up a design magazine or check out an interiors blog—but applying lagom to our homes is not about one specific look. There's no checklist for a home that incorporates elements of lagom. Applying balance to your space is first about identifying what it is about your space that is important to you.

The size and amount of objects has little to do with the feel of a home. There are plenty of garish, enormous houses filled with useless items to prove that point, and a small, modest space can feel much more like a home than a large, expensive house. "The falsehood of the notion that beauty in the home is only gained through wealth can be seen in, among other things, the many homes crammed with meaningless luxury items and art objects, where no deep-seated thirst for beauty or personal taste has selected the objects or given them the space they require to have an impact," wrote Key.

Everyone's space is different, and there is no one "right" design, but the essential of a lagom home is that balance between look and function. A home is meant to be used and to be loved. A home that's well designed is one that works for you and your family. It does not need to be expensive, or so perfect that it could land itself in the pages of a magazine in order for it to be well-used or loved. Even with the smallest, simplest of spaces we can create something that feels good to us, that is functional and meant to be used.

The homes of my Swedish friends and family always feel this way. There is never a room that isn't meant to be used, the sofas are inviting to sit on, and there's the general feeling that the people who live in the particular home have made it theirs. Certainly, many have elements of what we think of as typical "Swedish" design—wooden floors, white ceramic-tiled kitchens, a bright patterned textile to bring life into the room—but they are always unique and personal. "A room does not have a soul until someone's soul is revealed in it, until it shows us what that someone remembers and loves, and how that person lives and works every day," wrote Key.

In developing your own space, work with what you have. Achieving more balance in your home is not about going out and buying all the appropriate accoutrements. Instead, take a look at your space and identify what you love and what works, and what perhaps you might be able to live without. An old chair can be brought back to life with a throw put over it. A dark table can be brightened with a light-colored runner. A drab room can be enlivened with a potted plant.

Think about your own personal style first instead of simply incorporating elements of Swedish style that may not work in your own home. It's easy when attempting to bring a certain style into a home to overdo things, making a space quickly go from feeling unique and personal to a sterile showroom.

Cozy Interiors

Danish has *hygge*, and in Swedish the word *mysig* conveys a similar feeling of comfort and coziness. This is an integral part of Swedish design, a reflection of the importance of the home to be a welcoming, nurturing space.

Lighting is one way of doing that. As I have mentioned before, the dark Swedish winters beg for light and dictate much of Swedish architecture; spaces are designed to maximize the natural light. Because natural light is not always available, lighting fixtures are also essential, a space needing the perfect diffusion of light to bring comfort and beauty to a room. Light should be relaxing, not jarring. In the winter, a collection of candles can help to bring joy into a dark room; a lagom amount of lit candles in Sweden is definitely more than just a few.

A sense of coziness is also made through textiles and furniture, creating pleasant places to sit and congregate as a family or with friends. For example, in a living room, centering chairs and sofas around a coffee table, encouraging interaction, as opposed to all being turned towards a television. Designing with conviviality in mind helps to create an inviting space that we want to settle in to.

Detaching from Our Things

Just as we fill our schedules to the brim, we do the same with our houses. Our lives are busy and so are our homes. In today's world of mass consumption, it's easy to fall into the trap of regularly buying new things in the hope that they will spruce up our space. But this is a plaster, and a costly one at that (both to our own wallets and the environment).

Applying the concept of lagom to one's home for a balanced space means first and foremost going through that space to identify the things that we love and use. We want our homes to be functional, but also to bring us joy. So often our homes are filled with non-essentials. Sometimes that's because we're holding on to them out of guilt—that ugly vase your grandmother bought you—and other times it's because we think that one day we'll get good use out of them, like most kitchen appliances used only once and then pushed to the back of the cupboard.

Objects do not define us. It is the ideas, feelings, and experiences they facilitate that are important. Think about a dinner party. With the right group of friends and a good meal you can host a spectacular evening, even if you're eating off something as simple as paper plates. But if you have a stunning set of dinnerware, without those friends and food, it's not much more than a lonely, hungry evening with beautiful crockery. When we separate ourselves from objects, we reaffirm the importance of experiences and relationships.

Quality over Quantity

Quality over quantity is an important element at work, and it transfers over to the home. Today, it's easy to find a new table and a sofa for almost less than the price of a good meal out, and because they are cheap, there is not much stopping us from switching them when we tire of them. We live in a throwaway culture.

This all comes at a cost. With cheap materials and cheap goods comes cheap labor and cutting corners on environmental standards; society and the environment suffers. Today, as a global society we're consuming resources as if we had 1.6 planet Earths. Changing our attitudes isn't just an option, it's a necessity.

Cultivating an awareness, and appreciation, for good quality craftsmanship is not just about the look of products but also about their impact. Upfront, these products may have a more expensive price tag, but they are long-term investments, lasting for decades, and perhaps even generations, both in what they are made of and how they look. "Timelessness in the Nordic 'lagom' designs creates a safe style, since by definition they take longer to appear outdated and therefore don't have to be switched out as often," says Ramstedt. Today, we benefit from the well-made, timeless designs of several generations ago—the existence of vintage furniture is entirely dependent on that furniture being long-lasting. It's hard to imagine future generations coveting some of the cheap interior accoutrements that fill our homes today.

This attitude towards quality over quantity also comes with an attitude toward buying less. If you are investing in quality products, it means investing in a small amount of them. Over time, as you have built up the collection of products that you want in your home, you eventually don't need to buy more.

That goes counter to the culture that we currently live in, the one that tells us that our lives would be better if we bought yet more additional things. A sofa, a table, a lamp; it doesn't matter what it is, ultimately the item being sold is to fill a void. When you have created a home that you love, a life that's in balance where you feel, and know, that you have enough, that void gets smaller. The urge might never fully go away, we are surrounded after all with messaging about the importance of consumption, but being aware of that urge and how to say no to it is essential.

As you read this, I know that there is a question that comes to mind: "What about IKEA?" The Swedish retailer has become a global icon in home furnishings. Today we can easily find the same table in Manhattan, Sydney, and Singapore.

While today's version of the furniture company has created a culture of mass consumption of inexpensive products, the roots of the company are the same social principles guiding much of the rest of Swedish design; that good design makes life better and that it should be available to everyone. "I think that IKEA is an excellent example of Swedish 'democratic design,'" says Ramstedt.

Unfortunately, "democratic design" has come to be equated with excess; when products are overly cheap, it's hard to resist them, and whether it's furniture or clothing, the global production of cheap goods comes at a cost. But how we consume is up to us. Buying a kitchen table because we need one and we'll have it for years to come is different from buying a table that we'll swap out next year.

IKEA continues to be a leading company because it works to find a balance between good design, creativity, and price. Aware of its impact, IKEA has a large focus on sustainability through its "People & Planet Positive" initiative. In the UK, IKEA even instituted a Live Lagom campaign to encourage people to employ a variety of small changes in their everyday lives to help them live more sustainably.

Sustainability is an essential part of design moving forward. "Sustainability and health are two important aspects of design's future. We are really good about eating organic food, but don't care very much if we crawl into sheets made of cotton sprayed with pesticides or if we sleep in beds that are made with petroleum-based products that emit chemicals throughout the bed's lifetime," says Ramstedt. "Not to mention how much the production of disposable furniture wears on the environment. A lot of what we surround ourselves with in our homes contains strange materials, unnecessary chemicals and plastics, and this is where I think Sweden is going to be a leader in a lot of ways."

> With glass you are able to sculpt with light and with
> help from the sun you can paint with colors.
>
> SVEN PALMQVIST (SWEDISH GLASS DESIGNER)

INCORPORATING A LAGOM APPROACH TO DESIGN IN YOUR HOME

Taking inspiration from Swedish design, here are
ways to bring a more balanced approach to the design
in your home:

Simplicity of lines and forms
Swedish design is often thought of as clean and pared
back, an avoidance of anything that is inessential to
the object. What's needed is incorporated, and the
object is made to look beautiful, but often there are
not a lot of embellishments. There is a belief that there
is daily pleasure to be found in simple forms that are
not ostentatious.

Light
A Nordic country, Sweden is a dark place during the
winter months. To combat the darker days, interiors are

made to be light, often painted white or in neutral shades
that allow for a light space but also offer the chance to
add a pop of color that will stand out and bring some
energy into the room.

Open spaces
While Swedish homes have a variety of furniture, textiles,
and artwork, they never feel cluttered. There is room to
breathe, perhaps indicative of the Swedish love of nature
and landscapes. A Swedish room often feels like a breath
of fresh air.

Intimate
Swedish design is focused on the home and family—more
about the functionality and feel of a home than about
showing off to the outside world. Swedish homes are cozy,
inviting, a place you want to curl up in.

A natural space
Inspired by an appreciation for nature and the outdoors,
many Swedish prints and textiles feature botanicals. The
same goes for materials used. It is only in the last century
that synthetic materials hit the market and changed the

nature of the products that we use on a regular basis. Natural materials such as wool and wood are common in the Swedish home, and can feel like a welcome relief in a world of plastic. The natural materials common in Swedish homes are those that are local and specific to the region: a table made out of pine, a sheepskin used as a throw on the sofa, a basket made from birch bark, a glass vase to hold fresh flowers. When we use local materials in our design, we draw a deeper connection to the place in which we live.

Timeless designs

When we buy furniture that's trendy, there's an inherent risk that, eventually, it will go out of style. With significant, costly furniture items, consider more timeless designs, ones that you can have with you for your lifetime. When you are in need of a change, smaller objects, such as sofa cushions, dish towels, and other textiles, can be changed for more modern prints, bringing a good balance of design that lasts through the ages and more current styles.

LAGOM DESIGN ROOM BY ROOM

In the Swedish home, every room serves a purpose, each with its particular ambience. There is a sense of balance—while there are beautiful, well-designed objects, nothing is done for show and everything is meant to be used.

Kitchen

The kitchen is very much a family space in the Swedish household, a place to cook, eat, and spend time together. If a Swedish household has a separate dining room, often the kitchen will still feature a small table and perhaps a kitchen bench, used for simple meals and breakfast— the community center of the kitchen.

Five ways to bring lagom into your kitchen

- When it comes to objects in the kitchen, this is where form and function truly shine. Instead of filling the space with many single-use gadgets—basically anything sold under the guise of "revolutionizing" your kitchen— favor fewer simple, tried-and-true objects.

- Every Swedish kitchen has a good selection of textiles, including dish towels and wash cloths. Incorporate a mix of textiles made of natural fibers, such as cotton or linen. Include some in neutral colors and others in bright patterns. In the kitchen, botanical prints can be a perfect fit.
- Place your regularly used cooking utensils—wooden spoons, whisks, etc.—on the counter in a ceramic jug or glass jar. This makes them easily accessible when cooking as well as aesthetically pleasing.
- Sandwich boards and trays made from wood are great for open-faced sandwiches, which are a common Swedish food—be it for breakfast or an early afternoon snack.
- When it comes to tableware, opt mostly for items that can be used every day, mixing basic colors and some patterns. Pair these with a small selection of distinctive plates and glassware for more special occasions.

Living Room

Swedish living rooms are cozy and meant for relaxing, often with lots of accessories such as wool blankets and sheepskins—a nice balance between beautiful design and functionality. Like other rooms in the house, light and space are important—make the living room feel inviting and personal without having it feel cluttered. This is a space that you want to go to on a lazy weekend afternoon or in the evening after dinner to read a book curled up on the couch.

Five ways to bring lagom into your living room

- Mix textures, for example, by covering wood floors with rag rugs or covering a hard chair with a throw. If you have a space that's big on light colors and soft textures, bring in something that balances out the area, such as a metallic lighting fixture.
- Think about the focal point of the room; it doesn't have to be the television. Arrange the space so that it's conducive to any relaxing activity: reading, drawing, talking, or just sitting and looking out of the window.
- Books are a central part of a living room. Have a good permanent storage system for reading material, as well as something for the books and magazines that you are currently reading so that they aren't left lying around on the floor or chairs.

- If the living room is large, think about individual lighting fixtures next to each sitting place. This makes for a cozier, more personal feel than just having one central light.
- For living rooms that focus on more muted tones, bring in a few wild textiles such as sofa cushion covers, a blanket or even a wall hanging for a pop of color.

Bedroom

While sleeping means that you spend a lot of time in your bedroom, most people don't use the room for other purposes, which means that it doesn't need to be enormous. Your bedroom should be a place of calm and respite.

Five ways to bring lagom into your bedroom

- Think small. Your bedroom doesn't have to be spacious, in fact a small space can feel like a cozy nest, the perfect place to tuck into for the night.
- Keep the design simple. Your bedroom is a place for resting and rejuvenation; keeping a simple décor allows your brain to turn off after a long day.

- Create a space next to the bed, such as a shelf or night-stand, with good lighting and some simple storage for nighttime reading materials and a glass of water.
- Mix textures and patterns in your bedding. A set of simple cotton or linen sheets can be offset with a colorful blanket on top.
- A large open space can feel a little warmer with a large rug on the floor, perhaps partly under the bed.

ART AND CRAFT

Form follows function may have been the principle of the Modernist movement, but craftspeople in Sweden have been making objects to serve a function for centuries. Sweden arrived late to industrialization in comparison to other countries, but that industrialization was built on a long tradition of manufacturing that already existed, like with wood, textiles, and iron and steel products. Craftsmanship, and making things, was embedded into Swedish culture, and this structure helped to ensure that the craft traditions have carried on into modern-day Sweden.

Today, art and craft continues to hold a strong place in Swedish culture. The pursuit of Swedish craft is often more about the function than it is about the spectacle, returning to the idea that design can make our lives better, both through how we look at things and how we use them. That balance of function and aesthetic, tied with the tradition of craft in Sweden, results in bringing beauty to everyday objects—be it a rug, a pair of mittens, or a sweater.

However, not all artists identify with this need for "good design." I once read a quote from a Swedish artist

referring to artists being confined by the "straitjacket of good design," pointing out that there was more artistic freedom to create something wild in other countries. And yet, that Scandinavian restraint, the tendency to not go all the way to the extremes, is also what makes so much of Swedish art and craft beautiful.

One could argue that the Swedish art and craft scene is a representation of Slow Art, art that preserves the tradition of craft and puts a value on the time and energy spent to make something well. In fact, in 2013 the National Museum in Sweden hosted an exhibit titled *Slow Art*, showcasing over thirty pieces from its collection, including silver, textiles, glass, and ceramics, all mediums that require time and care. When we honor art and craft in this way, it is a reminder that in modernizing, we don't need to throw out the lessons and traditions of the past.

The textile arts are particularly revered in Sweden, traditions that have been handed down over the ages. Generations have knitted intricate, now iconic, designs into everyday items like sweaters and mittens. Weaving rugs from rags used to be a common household duty, an art form that grew out of having little and making do with what was available. Today, there is a new generation of women and men taking back these traditionally female crafts, helping to revive the art forms and give credit to the women rarely honored for their work and creativity.

There are many government and nonprofit initiatives to protect and promote crafts in Sweden, and the country is home to several internationally renowned design and art colleges. With such a push for the importance of craft, it's no surprise that, overall, culturally there's an importance put on making things.

We may not all be artists or craftspeople, but taking a cue from the Swedes and finding a broader appreciation for this domain can help us to find new value in old traditions.

Step away from technology
Technology serves a purpose, but it's essential for us to balance it by making things with our own hands. It's why there is meditation to be found in cooking. Consider learning a craft or making personal things from scratch for your home, friends, and family. Time invested in making things is not only good for our emotional well-being and creativity, but these end products can help to bring warmth into our daily lives.

Find a creative outlet that's right for you

Not everyone likes to draw, and not everyone likes to build things. But as humans, we have spent centuries making things with our hands and creating art that we put into the world. We have a primal need to make, and research shows that such activity is good for us, helping with our mental wellbeing. Be it writing, knitting, singing, woodworking, or blacksmithing, find the creative outlet that makes you feel good.

Commit to a longer-term project

It can be hard to bring creativity into our everyday lives. Challenge yourself with a goal like making something every day for thirty, even one hundred days. You may need to push yourself through it, but you'll come out the other end not only satisfied, but perhaps even with a new daily creative practice.

Invest in art and craft

If creating art is not your passion, support the people for whom it is. Part of cultivating a culture of art and craftsmanship means investing in it, even on a small scale. There is art available at all price ranges, and with the rise of the maker movement, it's becoming easier and easier to find handcrafted, local items. Consider supporting an independent artist next time you need to buy a birthday or Christmas present.

Simple Craft Projects for the Home

Here are ways to bring lagom arts and crafts into your home.

Felting sweaters

Old wool sweaters can get a second life by felting them. Wash the sweaters in hot water to turn them into felt. If you want the felt a little thicker, put the sweaters into a load with heavier clothing, like jeans, as this helps to agitate the wool. Once you have felted the sweaters, you have a new material to play with. Simple no-sew projects include coasters and hot pads for placing under a teapot. For a little more involved ideas, you can hand-sew items such as tea cosies, mittens, and even a pair of slippers.

Leaf bunting

Bring a little nature into your home or office by making a simple leaf bunting. Pick leaves with sturdy stems, then

use a strand of natural fiber string, like linen or hemp, to tie the stems on. Evenly spacing out the leaves along the string, you can make the bunting as long or as short as you want to. These are particularly beautiful in fall when the leaves change color.

Branch hooks
With a drill you can easily bring a little nature into your home with branch hooks. Bark can be left on the branch, or stripped depending on the look that you're going for. Stripped branches can be dried out then painted. Drill a hole (or several depending on the size of the branch) into the branch where you want the screws to go, then screw it into the wall. Thinner branches work best for this, and also make good hooks for smaller objects such as keys or a wool hat.

Printing with leaves
With leaves (and even branches and flowers) and fabric ink, you can design your own unique textiles. Ink a leaf, place it ink side down on a piece of fabric—dish towels, sheets, a shirt, pillowcases, the options are endless!—then

place a paper towel on top. Firmly press with your hand or roll with a brayer, then remove the leaf to reveal your print. Follow the instructions for the ink to set it.

Paper lampshades

Old lamps can be turned into new ones by making your own lampshades. Paper and cardboard are easy materials to work with and can be used in a variety of ways to make lampshades, from creating a simple, cylinder shade to more complicated, geometric styles of origami lampshades. If you are feeling particularly creative, you can print your own designs on lampshades or even do simple cut-outs to let the light shine through.

FASHION

Think of famous Swedish fashion designers: Filippa K, Acne Studios, Swedish Hasbeens, Nudie Jeans, Sandqvist. The aesthetic is simple, often pared down, with clean lines and classic designs that can be worn over time. We don't tend to associate flair with Swedish fashion as we might with other cultures, say France; while beautiful and noteworthy, Swedish clothing rarely screams "look at me." Yet at the same time, there is still an edge to Swedish fashion.

"Lagom is so much more than a word, it's a concept of living and has been with us since birth. Therefore it is rather hard to imagine fashion design without lagom," says Pim Sjöström, Production Manager of Nudie Jeans. "Ever since we were born we have been told to be lagom. But maybe because of this the Swedish people in general have been early adopters of avant-garde fashion. There is a small wish inside each of us to break through."

The Swedish wardrobe tends to be subdued. "We have a sober and rather clean wardrobe. The silhouettes are slimmer and all the colors are darker," says Sjöström. There are, as always, exceptions, like the wild and colorful

designs of Gudrun Sjödén, and as global fashion changes, so does Sweden's fashions, but the principles remain focused on quality, long-lasting items.

There is, of course, one exception. When it comes to clothing, Sweden is perhaps most well known for its fashion conglomerate H&M. Cheap fashion has made it easy to buy the latest trends, but it has come at a severe cost, socially and environmentally. Fast fashion is the antithesis of a lagom wardrobe, one that's filled with excess because of a cheap price point.

Just like bringing a more lagom approach to our home design, the same goes for what we wear, and our choices do have an impact. Here are some ways to rethink what you wear and what you buy:

Identify your style
Instead of having your wardrobe dictated by trends, identify a style that works for you and makes you feel good. Knowing what you love to wear makes it easier to shop for the right thing when you do need something new.

Invest in pieces that you love

It's easy to pick up a cheap T-shirt because of the price tag, but often this causes us to buy things we wear once or twice, or even worse, never. Think of the items hanging in your closet that have barely been worn. Instead of five pairs of trendy trousers, invest in one pair that you know you are going to wear. Identifying your style truly helps with this, as it allows you to easily filter out what you know isn't going to work in your wardrobe.

Combine function and style

The base of your wardrobe should be pieces that are versatile and can be rotated through a variety of everyday uses. Think of fashion like design; the balance between beauty and functionality.

A long-lasting wardrobe

There's no denying that clothes wear out, but let them wear out from use and not from fleeting trends. A more lagom wardrobe is one that is sensible yet fashionable and lasts for many seasons.

Choose consciously minded brands

Today, there are more and more designers and brands trying to shift the fashion needle towards designs that are increasingly ethical. Remember that all elements of fashion come at a cost—be it the pesticides used to grow the cotton for a shirt or the low wage paid to the person assembling shoes—and our choices do have a serious impact. Opt for brands doing the right thing.

FOOD AND DRINK

In Swedish, lagom is a word that is very often (perhaps even most often) used in association with food, a reminder of adequate portions and intake. How much salt should you have? A lagom amount. A popular brand of spreadable butter is called Lätt & Lagom (Light & Lagom), made with a blend of milk and rapeseed oil to reduce the fat content in comparison to regular butter. Lagom is a guiding principle in the Swedish kitchen.

When you think about it, the Swedish diet has always been pretty lagom. With a predominantly peasant history, the cuisine was born out of few ingredients and making use of the little that was available. This is not a country with an extravagant food culture. Meals are usually a one-dish affair, not like the multiple courses of somewhere like France. The ingredients are straightforward and simple, reflective of what's available in the Northern land. While that can at times be boring—in the middle of winter you can only eat so many root vegetables—it is also a reason why Swedish, and Scandinavian, cuisine has received so much attention in the last several years. As our attention has turned towards diets that are not only healthier but also more seasonally and geographically dictated, the simple culinary tradition is one to draw inspiration from. For the most part, the Swedish diet has consisted of whole grains and whole foods.

That is not to say that it's a cuisine that's solely focused on native ingredients. On the contrary, the harsh climate of Sweden has forced its inhabitants to look outward. It's one of the reasons why the Vikings set out to other lands. Trading was vital, not just for business reasons but to keep the population thriving. It's why exotic ingredients such as cardamom and cinnamon are staples of Swedish baked goods. Today, as Sweden has welcomed immigrants from different cultures around the world, new foods have entered into the Swedish culinary repertoire. Modern Swedish cooking is the combination of the best of both worlds, the lagom amount of inside and outside influence.

Swedish food is also no-fuss food. Even the fancier meals that might get served at holiday or celebration meals don't come with a long list of ingredients. Instead they depend on the quality of the fresh ingredients, and perhaps the addition of a few spices.

Balanced is a word that comes to mind when thinking about Swedish food, but not because it's a part of some health-food trend. Instead, it's because whole grains and produce have always been a part of the national diet. It was a country that for a long time had very little. The food that was made had to be full of sustenance, and nothing went to waste. Certainly that's changing today, as just as in most Western countries, there are more and more fast-food restaurants, more and more supermarkets selling prepackaged meals. But despite all of that, there is still an underlying appreciation of what good food and drink is.

Don't let the focus on fresh and simple ingredients lead you to believe that the Swedes don't know how to have fun. Far from it; if you have ever sat down at a Swedish café for an afternoon coffee, you'll know what I am talking about. Baked goods and pastries have a special importance in Swedish food culture—fresh cinnamon buns pulled from the oven, a sticky chocolate cake served at an afternoon with friends. Coffee breaks can extend for hours and Friday night dinner parties can last long into the night. This is, after all, the land of aquavit.

Writer, chef, and author of *How to Hygge*, Signe Johansen, often refers to this as "healthy hedonism," the idea that a little enjoyment every so often is an essential part of a healthy lifestyle. A lagom amount of sensible food and drink, and a lagom amount of the fun stuff.

Fika

It's impossible to write a book about Swedish culture without mentioning fika. In fact, you may remember it from the chapter on work culture. Fika is the iconic Swedish coffee break. As a word, it can be used as both a noun and a verb, and it indicates the moment in the day when you pause for a coffee and perhaps a little something to eat with it. It doesn't have to be coffee, you can enjoy a cup of tea as well, but the essential part is the break. Often, fika is enjoyed with friends, or co-workers, and is an excuse to catch up and socialize. Most importantly, fika is a break, the chance to take a few moments of respite from the day. It's an excuse to make time to check out from your routine for a few moments, enjoy a cup of coffee and just be.

Holidays

Just as there's a lagom approach to eating, there's also
a lagom approach to lagom itself, for there are several
times in the year to overindulge in Swedish food and
drink. Christmas and Midsummer are excellent examples.
The traditional dinners for both holidays are full of
a variety of foods and celebratory moments to let go
of the expectations of proper amounts of food and drink.
The *julbord*, or Christmas table, features a large spread
of many dishes, from meatballs to pickled herring to
salads. And that's just the savory spread. The month
of December is full of sweet treats like *pepparkakor*,
Swedish gingerbread cookies, sweet saffron buns, and
glögg, Swedish mulled wine.

At Midsummer, the Swedish celebration of the
summer solstice, it's the summer produce that's on display.
Cakes are topped with fresh strawberries, cooked salmon
is served with potatoes and dill, and the aquavit-fuelled
dinner extends late into the night, as this far north the
sun barely sets.

The Swedish Pantry

If you're looking to incorporate a more lagom approach
to eating into your every day, here are the core

components of a Swedish pantry. The basics of Swedish cuisine are whole foods and fresh, local ingredients, so adapt your pantry based on where you live and what's available.

Whole grains
While the modern Swedish diet has come to incorporate processed white flour, traditional whole grains are still sought after, while recently traditional baking methods and local foods have begun to increase in popularity. Rye has always been a popular grain in the North, coming to the Scandinavian countries by way of Russia. You'll find it in Swedish bread as well as in porridge form. Barley and oats are also common.

Dairy
Smör och bröd gör kinden röd goes an old Swedish saying, which translates to "Butter and bread makes the cheek red." In fact, even the name for sandwich includes the word butter, *smörgås*, which translates to "butter goose." Butter and cream are regular ingredients in many staple dishes, both sweet and savory. Fermented dairy products like yogurt and *filmjölk* (a thick sour milk that's similar

to kefir) are common on the breakfast table. Eggs are also incorporated into many Swedish dishes, as well as eaten on their own. A simple lunch can be a soft-boiled egg with a piece of *knäckebröd*, "crispbread," spread with butter and topped with a slice of cheese. Today of course there are more and more people who opt out of dairy, either for dietary or personal reasons. This has increased the level of non-dairy alternatives, like oat-based milk products.

Seasonal, fresh produce
Today, thanks to supermarkets, Swedes have the luxury of year-round access to fresh produce. This wasn't always the case and, as such, a lot of traditional Swedish foods are based around what's available seasonally. In the winter, that means lots of root vegetables, such as potatoes, parsnips, carrots, and beetroot. In the summer, Sweden is a land of abundance, with flavorful berries, fresh herbs, and lots of greens.

Fish and meat
Fish is, and has always been, a staple of the Swedish diet, particularly in a country where fresh vegetables

weren't available for many months out of the year and the population needed sustenance. Local varieties like herring, mackerel, trout, and whitefish are common. Pickling fish is a traditional preservation method and visitors to Sweden will likely encounter *sill*, "pickled herring," commonly served with a side of *snaps*, "aquavit." Pork, lamb, and beef are all regular ingredients in Swedish entrées, one of the more well-known ones being meatballs. Today there is a growing population of vegetarians and even those who don't stick to a vegetarian diet try to limit their intake of meat. Swedish schools often offer a vegetarian alternative at meals and many even offer a "meat-free" day.

Local, organic, and environmentally friendly
Whether it's a locally produced item or organic produce, there is a general consciousness toward where food comes from and the impact that it has. This is not to say that Swedish grocery shopping is without its contradictions— the organic sections are regularly full of foods imported from far away, for example. But in general, there is an inclination toward ingredients that are produced in an ethical way, both for people and for the environment.

MAKING SWEDISH FOOD AT HOME

This isn't a cookery book, but it felt like cheating you, dear reader, if I didn't include a few recipes. I grew up in the kitchen helping my mother, always making meals from scratch with simple ingredients. Growing up in the United States in the 1980s, this was far from the norm—friends were eating multicolored cereals while I had breakfasts of tea and open-faced sandwiches.

Swedish-inspired food is a part of my everyday routine, and I am guided by the principles of simple meals made with seasonal, local ingredients. Here are some of my favorite recipes that embody this Swedish approach to eating. They all have easy ingredients and a quintessential Swedish taste. Some are on the healthier side, some a little more indulgent. These capture the essence of the Swedish kitchen—food that is grounding and part of an overall healthy approach to living.

Råglimpor—Rye loaves

This recipe is inspired by a classic recipe for Swedish *limpa*, a sweet bread made from rye flour and spiced with caraway and anise. I make my version with honey and a little more rye flour so that it has a denser consistency.

Makes 2 loaves

2 teaspoons active dry yeast
2 tablespoons honey
2 cups (480 ml) warm water, plus 2 tablespoons
2 teaspoons fennel seeds
1 teaspoon anise seeds
1 teaspoon caraway seeds
½ teaspoon salt
Zest of 1 small orange
2 ½ cups (350 g) rye flour, plus extra as needed
1 ¼ cups (175 g) wholemeal flour
1 ¼ cups (185 g) plain flour
Olive oil, for greasing

Place the yeast and the honey in a small bowl. Add the 2 tablespoons of warm water and mix. Let sit for 10 minutes until the yeast has dissolved and starts to bubble.

After the yeast has proofed, add it to a large bowl with the rest of the water, fennel, anise, caraway, salt, and orange zest. Add in the flours a little bit at a time, gradually stirring and working the dough together. When you have added all the flours, you should be able to work it into a solid dough.

Gently knead the dough on a floured work surface for about 3–5 minutes. The dough should feel moist, but keep your rye flour bag close so that if the dough sticks too much to your fingers you can add a little bit. Note that this dough has a tendency to be sticky, but you don't want to overdo it on extra flour, so knead a few times and then use a spatula to scrape it off the flat surface, before kneading a few more times. This will keep you from having a crazy, sticky mess.

Form the dough into a ball and place back in the bowl. Cover with a tea towel and let sit for about an hour to rise.

When the dough has risen, prepare a baking tray smeared with a little olive oil. Separate the dough into two even sections. With the first section, gently flatten it and form it into a rectangle, then fold it into thirds. Once folded into thirds, roll it into a log about 10–12 inches long. Place on the baking tray and repeat with the rest of the dough.

Place a tea towel over the loaves and let rise for another 45 minutes.

Towards the end of the rise, preheat the oven to 400°F/200°C.

When the loaves have risen, bake for 35–40 minutes until the loaves are a dark brown.

Remove from the oven and transfer to a cooling rack. Once cool, wrap in a tea towel to store.

Smörgås

Perhaps the most common food in Sweden are open-faced sandwiches. They are easy to make, and can be done with an infinite combination of *pålägg*, "sandwich toppings."

Suggested pålägg combinations:

- Butter and thin cheese slices (to this you can add thinly sliced vegetables or fruit, such as cucumbers, radishes, red peppers, apples, or pears)
- Herb butter and sliced egg
- Mayonnaise, small prawns, and dill
- Sliced meatballs (also works well with a vegetarian version) and pickled beetroot
- Cured salmon and a mustard dill sauce

Knäckebröd—Crispbread

Knäckebröd is a Swedish essential, served alongside almost every meal. Crispbread has been baked for centuries and is traditionally made with rye flour and baked with a hole in the center so that it could be hung up on a rod and stored through the winter. Swedes eat several kilos of knäckebröd every year. This version is made with baking powder instead of yeast, which simplifies the baking process. The trick is to roll these as thin as you can for a nice crispy finish. Serve them in a basket along with a little butter and cheese at dinner time or for a simple lunch eat with a hard-boiled egg.

Makes 10–12 crispbread

1 cup (250 g) plain yogurt
⅓ cup (80 ml) oil (for a more neutral taste opt for rapeseed oil—olive oil works fine too), plus extra for greasing
1 teaspoon baking powder
1 teaspoon anise seeds
2 teaspoons caraway seeds
¼ teaspoon salt
1 cup (140 g) rye flour, plus extra as needed
1 cup (150 g) wholemeal flour

Preheat the oven to 400°F/200°C.

In a bowl, mix together the yogurt and oil until well blended.

In a separate bowl, combine the dry ingredients. Slowly add the dry ingredients to the wet mixture, mixing until a dough forms.

Separate the dough into 10–12 small balls, about the size of walnuts. On a floured surface, roll out the balls as thin as you can get them.

Grease two baking trays with olive oil (you will have to bake these in several rounds). Bake the crispbreads for 10–12 minutes, until they are a deep golden brown. The baking time will depend on how thick you roll them—you may need to bake them for more or less time.

Remove from the oven and let cool for a few minutes before moving to a cooling rack. Once completely cool, stack together and store in an airtight container.

Inlagd gurka med dill—Dill-marinated cucumber
These marinated cucumbers are both sweet and vinegary
and accented by fresh dill. They are perfect for using
atop a sandwich or served alongside a meal. You can
experiment with other herbs as well—chopped mint
and cilantro are great additions. You can also swap
honey for the sugar, which adds a bit of a deeper flavor.

Serves 7–10

1 cup (240 ml) water
4 tablespoons natural cane sugar
4 tablespoons white wine vinegar
Pinch of salt and freshly ground black pepper
1 large cucumber, very thinly sliced
1 tablespoon chopped fresh dill

In a large clean jar, combine the water, sugar, vinegar,
salt, and pepper. Place a lid on the jar and shake until the
sugar is mostly dissolved.

Add the sliced cucumbers and dill and push the
cucumbers down so that they are covered in the liquid.

Let sit in the refrigerator for at least an hour before
eating. Stores for up to a week.

Linssallad med rödbetor och feta ost
—Beetroot, lentil, and feta salad

This is a salad that can be served warm or cold, and with lentils it is hearty enough to stand alone as a simple meal. If eaten on its own, it makes three to four big portions. If served as a side dish, it will serve a few more. For some extra texture, toss in a handful of toasted walnuts.

Serves 3–4 as an entrée

Salad
4 medium-sized beetroots
Pinch of salt
1 cup (200 g) green lentils
2 cups (480 ml) water
1 shallot, thinly sliced
7 ounces feta cheese
Orange zest, to garnish

Dressing
2 tablespoons balsamic vinegar
4 tablespoons olive oil
Juice of 1 orange
Salt and freshly ground black pepper

Place the beetroots in a saucepan and cover with water. Add a little salt and bring to a boil. Reduce the heat to medium-low and let cook for about 30–45 minutes, until they are tender. The cooking time will depend on the size of the beetroots. To expedite the cooking time, you can also halve or quarter the beetroots. Once the beetroots have cooked, rinse them with cold water. When they have cooled enough to touch, peel the skin using a knife.

While the beetroots are cooking, place the lentils and the water in a saucepan and bring to a boil. Reduce the heat and let simmer, uncovered, until the lentils have softened, about 20–30 minutes. The water level should just barely cover the lentils. Add more water if needed. When the lentils are cooked, pour off any leftover water.

Place the cooked lentils in a large bowl. Cut the beetroots into small cubes and add to the bowl along with the thinly sliced shallot and the feta cheese, crumbled into small pieces. Mix together.

To make the dressing, place the ingredients in a bowl and whisk together. Alternatively, you can place in a jar and shake together. Pour over the salad and toss together. Garnish with orange zest.

Potatisgratäng med purjolök och svamp
—Potato, leek, and mushroom gratin

Potato gratins are common Swedish side dishes, particularly in the midst of winter. This one brings some additional seasonal flavor with the help of leeks and mushrooms. Any mushroom will work for this dish, and maybe you're even lucky enough to have access to wild ones.

Serves 4–6

2 tablespoons olive oil, plus extra for greasing
1 garlic clove, finely chopped
1 large leek, rinsed and sliced
3 cups (125 g) mushrooms, sliced
3–4 large potatoes (about 2 kg)
½ cup (70 g) hazelnuts, chopped
Salt and freshly ground black pepper
1 cup (240 ml) double cream, plus extra as needed

Preheat the oven to 400°F/200°C.

In a frying pan over a medium heat, sauté the olive oil and chopped garlic until golden brown. Add the sliced leek and sauté until the leek starts to soften. Add the mushrooms and sauté until the mushrooms have started to decrease in size.

Halve the potatoes, then thinly slice them about ⅛-inch thick.

Grease a rectangular baking dish with olive oil and spread half of the potatoes evenly across the bottom. Cover the layer with the leeks, mushrooms, and hazelnuts. Season with salt and pepper. Layer the rest of the sliced potatoes on top, then cover with the cream and season with additional salt and pepper.

Bake for about 40–50 minutes. Check after about 30 minutes—if the dish looks dry on top, pour in a little more cream.

Remove from the oven and let cool for a few minutes before serving.

Päronkompott med Kardemumma
—Pear and cardamom compote
Fruit compote is a common way to use fruit in Sweden.
It's as simple as a little fruit and sweetener (either sugar or
honey) cooked down until soft. You can add a variety
of spices to heighten the flavor, such as cinnamon or
citrus peel. Here I've added my favorite spice, cardamom.
Compote can be served a variety of ways. For breakfast,
try a couple of spoonfuls in a bowl of yogurt. For dessert,
pair with whipped cream and sliced almonds or even
a little grated almond paste. You can also use it as a filling
for the Filled cardamom quick buns (page 169) or the
Pancake cake (page 165).

Makes about 2 cups (450 g)

2 large pears (about 500 g)
2 tablespoons honey
1 ½ teaspoons cardamom seeds, crushed

Wash the pears, then slice and cube them into small
pieces. Add them to a saucepan along with the honey
and crushed cardamom seeds.

Place over medium heat and stir regularly until some liquid has developed at the bottom and is bubbling. Reduce the heat to medium–low, cover and cook for about 15–20 minutes, until the pear is soft enough to mash with a fork.

Spoon the compote into a clean glass jar and cover with a lid. Let cool, then store in the refrigerator for up to 2 weeks.

Ostkaka—Swedish cheesecake

Let's get one thing straight: Swedish *ostkaka* has nothing to do with the Anglophone cheesecake. This old recipe hails from the dairy-farm-rich region of Småland, and was traditionally made by mixing milk with rennet. More modern versions use cottage cheese. The result is an egg bake that has a strong cheese flavor. It's traditionally served with whipped cream and *hjortonsylt*, "cloudberry jam." The sweet jam contrasts with the cheese flavor, similar to how you might serve sliced pears with a blue cheese for dessert. This *ostkaka* is also good drizzled with a little lime juice over the top.

Makes 1 cake

4 eggs
2 tablespoons honey
1 ¼ cups (300 ml) milk
2 cups (450 g) cottage cheese
½ cup (60 g) finely ground almonds or almond meal
Butter, for greasing

To serve
Whipped cream
Jam

Preheat the oven to 350°F/175°C.

In a bowl, whisk together the eggs and honey, then add in the rest of the ingredients and mix together until well blended.

Butter a baking dish and pour in the batter. Bake for 35–45 minutes, until a deep golden brown. Let cool a bit before serving with the cream and jam. You can also serve completely cold.

Pannkakor—Swedish pancakes

Pancakes are a simple, pleasurable food, popular with both children and adults. They are commonly served with jam and then rolled up. Any fruit compote works well with them, and they can also serve as a base for savory fillings, like sautéed greens and a sharp cheese.

Serves 3–4

3 eggs
2 ½ cups (600 ml) milk
½ cup (75 g) wholemeal flour
½ cup (70 g) plain flour
½ teaspoon salt
2 tablespoons unsalted butter, melted, plus extra for frying

In a bowl, whisk together the eggs and half of the milk. Stir in the flours and salt and whisk together. Add in the rest of the milk and whisk until smooth. Add the melted butter.

Place a cast-iron or non-stick frying pan on a medium–high heat. Add a little bit of butter to the pan to grease it. Pour in enough batter to thinly coat the bottom of the pan, if necessary tilting the pan to get the batter to spread out. Cook until the pancake has set, then carefully flip over and cook for a couple of minutes on the other side until a light golden brown.

Remove from the pan, place on a plate and serve immediately. Repeat with the rest of the batter.

Pannkakstårta—Pancake cake

I like to joke that *pannkakstårta* is the least lagom of
Swedish recipes. Thin pancakes are layered with whipped
cream and jam, or perhaps a fruit compote, resulting
in a decadent dessert. It's a common feature at children's
birthday parties, and even the subject of a children's
book by Swedish illustrator and author Sven Nordqvist.
But the beauty of such a recipe is that it's not for the
everyday; it's for special occasions when there's reason
to indulge—a classic example of healthy hedonism. In
the summer, I love to layer this cake with fresh berries.
In the winter, when fresh berries aren't an option, I use
frozen berries to do a simple fruit compote sweetened
with honey—usually a combination of blueberries
and raspberries. You can also use jam.

Makes 1 cake

1 batch of Swedish pancakes (page 163)
Jam or fruit compote
1–1½ cups (240–360 ml) double cream, whipped

Prepare the pancakes and let them cool.

Once cool, take a pancake and place it on a plate or cake tray. Spread with jam or fruit compote. Spread a thin layer of cream on top. Take another pancake and layer on top. Spread with jam or fruit compote and then the cream. Repeat until you have used all of the pancakes. Top with more whipped cream and fresh fruit or fruit compote. Serve immediately.

Fyllda Hastbullar—Filled cardamom quick buns

A proper fika will have some sort of baked good, and the most classic is cardamom buns. But you don't always have time to make a yeasted dough, and *hastbullar* are the perfect solution for whipping up quick fika treats. I make this version using ground almonds and brown rice flour, which makes them a nice gluten-free alternative. If you have a food processor at home, you can make the ground almonds yourself, or even try a version with hazelnuts. These are spiced with cardamom and to make them extra special are filled with either jam or a butter/cinnamon mixture, just as you would find in typical cinnamon or cardamom buns. Try the Pear and cardamom compote (page 157) for a filling, or any jam that you have on hand. Fresh berries will also work well—just mash them with a little sugar before placing in the buns.

Makes 12 buns

1 ½ cups (160 g) finely ground almonds or almond meal
1 ¼ cups (180 g) rice flour (or swap for half plain and half wholemeal flours)
¼ cup (55 g) sugar
3 teaspoons baking powder

1 ½ teaspoons cardamom seeds, crushed
7 tablespoons (100 g) butter
1 egg
½ cup (140 g) plain yogurt

Filling
About ⅓ cup (100 g) jam
Or
3 ½ tablespoons (50 g) butter, at room temperature
2 teaspoons ground cinnamon
1 teaspoon crushed cardamom seeds

Topping
Pearl sugar (optional)

Preheat the oven to 450°F/225°C.

In a bowl, mix together the almonds, rice flour, sugar, baking powder, and cardamom seeds. Cut the butter into the mixture in small cubes and work together with your fingertips until the mixture resembles coarse breadcrumbs.

In a separate bowl, whisk together the egg and yogurt. Add to the dry mixture and work together until a dough forms.

Spoon the dough into silicone or paper muffin liners. Using your finger or the back of a spoon, make an indent in the middle of each one. Place about a teaspoon of the jam into the indent or mix together the butter, cinnamon, and cardamom and add a teaspoon of this filling. Sprinkle with pearl sugar, if using.

Bake for 12–15 minutes until the tops are a deep golden brown.

Remove from the oven and let cool for a bit. Serve warm or let cool completely, then store in an airtight container.

LAGOM FOR HEALTH

Lagom is both a mental and physical state of being. It's easy to think of lagom as cutting out and cutting back. But an approach that involves moderation is less about focusing on the things that we don't have and instead appreciating what we do have. It's a celebration of a balanced way of living.

In the modern world, we're constantly looking for the quick fix to wellness. "If only I [insert revolutionary activity here], I will feel better." There is, however, no quick fix. Wellness is a balance between physical and mental health, figuring out what works for us and constantly adapting accordingly. What feels in balance one year may change the next. There is no simple formula. However, if we construct our lives in a more intentional way, being aware of ourselves, our surroundings, and our expectations, and start removing all of the non-essential items (both physically and emotionally), we can begin to find a constant happiness with who we are, not who we hope to become.

Our modern world is a constant reminder of everything that we have to be grateful for. Health, a home, a job, peace; these are considered luxuries by many in the world. It would be a shame to take those things for granted, and a shame to not be able to take advantage of the world around us because we are suffering physically and emotionally.

Health and wellness requires a holistic approach, finding a balance between the body and mind. You might spend five days a week training for a marathon, but if you continue to eat poorly and work in a stressful situation, your body will likely suffer. We all could use a lagom amount of activities that keep our bodies and mind healthy, not sacrificing one for the other.

MIND

Living in the now

We are constantly focused on the future, whether it's a trip we're taking, a promotion we're hoping to get or a house we want to buy. We are often so driven by our goals that they become inhibiting, keeping us from experiencing and enjoying the present. Incorporate more activities into your everyday routine that will keep you in the present. That can be a walk in the woods, a coffee break, or working on an art project. Celebrate the everyday. Spending time in the present allows us to be content with the now, instead of hoping for what's to come in the future.

Minimizing mental clutter

We often think of minimizing in respect to our belongings, but what about all of that mental clutter? Regret, anger, frustrations, envy; these are all emotions that take up space, and can get in the way of living. Just as our belongings don't magically disappear, neither does our mental clutter, and we have to intentionally work at getting rid of it. The process is the same as with our physical things:

assess what you need and don't need, then plan your strategy of ridding yourself of the non-essentials. This can be harder than actual clutter, because often it means diving deep into ourselves and our emotions. Which relationships feel draining to you? What is holding you back emotionally? Is there a daily task that's causing you anxiety? What negative feelings are you holding on to and where are they coming from? Only when we assess the situation can we make a strategy for dealing with our mental clutter and, hopefully, clean it out.

Unplugging

Be it emails, television, or texts, there is a lot in our everyday lives requiring our attention, and while these things all have their place, too much of them comes at a cost. Our minds need time unplugged, time with family, time with friends. Work on building unplugged time into your day, particularly in the evening before you go to bed. Avoid screens an hour or two before bed; use that time to read or spend time together as a family. Think of emails that need to be sent or computer tasks that need to be done. Keep a piece of paper or notebook on hand to jot those down and take care of them in the morning.

Connecting less online and connecting more in person
For many of us, social media has become a regular
part of our everyday routine. It's an easy way to stay
connected, but at the same time, it can easily cause
anxiety. Instead of relating to someone, we compare
ourselves to them. We present our best selves online,
something we often forget when we see an image of
a friend on their latest beautiful vacation; they probably
didn't post a photo the week before they left and were
stressed out at work trying to meet a deadline. We're
also connected to far more people than we would be
in real life, inundated with their stories, their trials and
tribulations. Robin Dunbar, a British anthropologist,
is often cited for coming up with Dunbar's number,
the cognitive limit to the amount of people with whom
we are able to maintain relationships. Dunbar puts
that number at 150. In that network of relationships,
which includes both more personal contacts as well
as general acquaintances, the number of close friendships
that we can manage is even smaller, somewhere around
five, according to Dunbar's research. Our brains, in other
words, aren't capable of handling the huge social
networks that we plug into on a daily basis, which makes
real time spent with friends essential.

Making time for solitude

Just as we need to make time for friends, we also need to make time for ourselves. Solitude allows us space to think, to reflect, to unwind, to avoid outer influences. In our ever-connected world, we are rarely alone, and when we are it can be easy to do things that keep us social, like emailing and texting. This doesn't mean you need to walk into the wild woods for a week, but do something that allows you to tune out the rest of the world. Give yourself the space for solitude.

Self-care

It's easy to be so focused on the wellbeing of others that we forget about ourselves. Pair that with the fact that society instructs us, particularly women, that we shouldn't be inward focused and it's easy to lose track of our own wellbeing. But to take care of others, to be a good colleague, a good community member, a good friend, we must be mindful of how we're doing. Schedule in time, even if it's the tiniest amount, just for you. It can be as simple as a still moment with a cup of tea, or a lunch out by yourself. Take care of yourself so that you can take care of others.

Managing stress

Chronic stress is not only linked to anxiety, depression, and sleep problems, but also to some of the leading causes of death, like heart disease. Managing stress is one of the most important things that we can do when it comes to not just our mental wellbeing, but our physical wellbeing as well. The Swedes don't have this one nailed down either—burn-out rates and stress levels are high these days. It's something that we can all work on. Managing our workloads and expectations is a start; remind yourself that it's OK to be "good enough" instead of striving for absolute perfection. Take time in your day to do an activity like yoga or meditation, even if it's just five minutes of focused breathing.

BODY

Wellness is about balance
Diets and weight-loss plans have come to be the norm
in a culture of excess. We work long hours, cram in
meals and make little time for taking care of our
systems. The response to this general cultural appetite
for excess has been met with more excess. Crash diets,
extreme addictions to fitness; we live on an either/
or scale. But our bodies crave balance. When thinking
about our physical health, it's important to remember
this and to remind ourselves that a healthy body requires
a holistic approach.

Build daily activity into your routine
Physical activity has always been an integral part of
Swedish culture. Part of that is thanks to an infrastruc-
ture that supports regular activity, like cycling to work
or walking and using public transportation. It's these
activities, paired with a love of the outdoors, that make
up the overall approach to healthy living in Sweden.
Think about how you might be able to build physical
activity into your everyday routine. Perhaps it means

not taking a bus for part of your commute to work and walking instead. Perhaps it means taking a stroll in the neighborhood during your lunch break. Perhaps it's doing more garden work. We don't have to spend time at the gym in order to be active.

Avoid long periods of sedentary activity
Even if you're a highly active person, going to work and sitting for several hours straight takes a significant toll. Our bodies don't just need an hour workout, they need general movement throughout the day to keep us strong and healthy. At work, incorporate small changes like stretches that can be done continually through the day during breaks. Take your meeting with a colleague outside, on a walk.

Embrace enjoyment
We're quick to demonize the things we "shouldn't" do. "Oh, I really shouldn't eat this, but . . ." If we allow ourselves to have a healthy amount of the things that feel good, we can enjoy them instead. If you're on a workout

plan and skip a day, enjoy that day off instead of thinking "I really should be exercising right now." If you indulge in a rich meal, turn the focus from the calories involved to the feeling of sharing a great meal with friends, and know that a rich meal every day probably isn't your best health choice, but one that every once in a while won't do much harm.

LAGOM AND THE ENVIRONMENT

> If anyone asks me what I remember from my childhood, my first thought is actually not of the people, but of that beautiful environment which framed my days then and filled them with such intensity, that as a grown-up you can hardly comprehend it. Wild strawberries among the rocks, carpets of blue spring flowers, meadows full of cowslips, special places where blueberries could be found, the forest where dainty pink flowers were nestling in the moss, the paddocks around Näs where we knew every little path and every little stone, the creek with the water lilies, ditches, streams, and trees—I remember all this more than the people.
>
> ASTRID LINDGREN

NATURE

Nature is inextricably linked to our wellbeing, both physically and mentally. Nature is our life force. For thousands of years we have lived in balance with the natural world, with a deep understanding of the world around us. We have adapted to our surroundings and the seasons.

The Swedish environment is one of extremes: sparse, dark, and cold in the winter, flourishing and full of light in the summer. The hardships of the landscape shaped the population. There was no choice but to adapt to the world around them; nature dictated behavior. Today, when modern conveniences like heating and lighting make it easier to get through the harsh winters, there is still a deep respect for nature. The outdoor world is very much a part of the Swedish psyche. In the summer, city dwellers escape to summer cabins, often nestled away from metropolises on the edge of a lake, in the heart of a forest—everyday summer living pared down to just the essentials. Foraging for wild foods is practically a national pastime—abundant wild strawberries and blueberries in the summer; chanterelles (often referred to as *skogsguld*, "forest gold") and other wild mushrooms hidden in the damp, mossy fall forest floor. Whatever season it is, picking food from the wild feels like winning the lottery.

In Sweden, time spent outside is time well spent, be it on a simple spring weekend walk in the forest or a week of skiing in winter. The Swedes are on to something.

There is a growing body of research that shows how much we suffer when we don't have exposure to the outdoor world. Writer Richard Louv is known for coining the term Nature Deficit Disorder, specifically focusing on the negative effects that children experience because they are so plugged into electronic devices instead of spending time outside. If we don't have enough nature in our lives, we don't thrive.

The physical and mental benefits that come from a connection to nature have led many to advocate all kinds of programs that get people outside. From Japan we have learnt the concept of "forest bathing," being in the midst of trees, and the benefits that can be gleaned from it, spawning a growing movement of forest therapy and eco-therapy. Nature is the antidote to many of the symptoms of our modern lives.

The good news, of course, is that nature is all around us, and we could all benefit from a little more of it in our everyday routines.

Reduce mental fatigue
Know that feeling of fatigue that comes from working or studying long hours? When you start being distracted and forgetful? Time spent in nature can help with

that, restoring the mind and making you feel alert and productive again. So instead of another cup of coffee, consider a walk.

Alleviating depression
More time spent outdoors can help to reduce depression, and one study has even shown that in some cases, exercise could be just as effective as anti-depressants.

Stress relief
Time outdoors can help to improve our mood and reduce our stress levels. Studies have shown that people who live near trees and parks have reduced levels of cortisol (a stress hormone). But these mental benefits of nature even stretch indoors. In one study of office spaces, workers with a window view of the forest felt less stress and increased job satisfaction.

Improving social connections
Urban planners are beginning to consider the benefits of nature as well. Green spaces like community gardens help to bring a community together, as well as offer the many benefits of spending time outside.

Nature vs. the Gym

When it comes to the health of our bodies, we usually think of fitness, and if we do, we most often end up thinking of a gym. Gyms are our modern, concrete world's answer to getting the daily required amount of movement. Not so long ago, the lifestyles of our ancestors kept them active and in good health, but today we have created a modern form of living that is predominantly sedentary. Physical activity is no longer built into our everyday life, and instead we must seek it out.

That's where the gym comes in; it's an easy place to go and be active. If you're not a gym-inclined person, you may squirm at the idea, the thought of spending an hour a few days a week among heavy machinery and sweaty strangers. But a large part of the population is gym obsessed. Yet despite a growing fitness industry, we're failing at becoming healthier. It's time we got outside.

Research shows that the benefits of outdoor exercise are hard to replicate indoors, and we could all benefit from taking our fitness routines outside, be it on a run, a bike ride, a yoga practice, or a walk.

For some, particularly those in the heart of an urban metropolis or in the heart of winter when you're hard pressed to be outside, the gym is often the best answer to getting in physical activity. When it is, even opting for the treadmill with a view of the outside world can be beneficial.

However, no matter where you live, there is usually some kind of outdoor access, even if it's as small as a park. An hour-long walk outside does a world of good, a restorative practice that keeps your body active and helps to reset your mind.

Nature Reminds Us of Who and Where We Are

A walk through a forest can be a restorative experience. Often, it's the chance to be alone with our own footsteps. Spend a day alone among the trees or at the water's edge and we are quickly reminded of our place in the world.

In nature, we are grounded and we have the opportunity to feel a part of something large above and beyond ourselves. Spending time in nature connects us to the world around us, reminding us that we are not just individuals, but part of a whole. We take part in a natural rhythm that's different from our own, one dictated by weather and light as opposed to a clock. The stress of that deadline or that meeting can easily fall away when nature causes us to look at the bigger picture.

Experiencing nature can be a solitary experience, but even when it is, because it helps to remind us of who and where we are, remind us that we are connected to everything around us, it can help to grow our appreciation for community and the common good.

Nature in All Seasons

Nature is a magical force, as every day there are new changes. A bare tree grows her buds in the springtime, is dressed in bright green leaves in the summer, and sheds her colors in the fall. Watching the seasons evolve, being a part of the natural cycles, that's an experience that we can't get from anywhere else.

There is enjoyment to be found in the outdoors in any season, and energy to be drawn from it. We think of winter as a time to hunker down, sit around the fireplace, stay indoors. In our modern world, we have the luxury of being able to escape the reality of winter. But that shouldn't stop us experiencing it. Swedes have a love of winter sports, like cross-country skiing and long-distance ice skating, activities that keep them in tune with what's happening in the outside world.

When we spend time outside we are also more likely to work to protect it. We cannot fight for something that we don't know, and becoming intimate with nature turns us into better advocates for it. Sustainability becomes less of a policy buzzword and more of a mindset. We make nature a part of our value system.

Bringing Nature Inside

We can't spend all of our time outside, but we can bring the outdoors indoors. Swedes have an affinity for bringing plants and flowers into their home, and following their lead can provide a host of benefits.

Grow an indoor kitchen garden

An easy way to bring more greenery into your home is to have a kitchen garden. This can be as simple as a few pots of fresh herbs. They will brighten the kitchen and your meals. Place a few pots of things like rosemary, thyme, oregano, and basil on your kitchen windowsill.

Potted plants

Short of opening a greenhouse, you can't overdo it when it comes to plants indoors. Not only are they a beautiful way to decorate, but they also have health benefits, such as increasing oxygen levels and purifying the air, as well as improving concentration and productivity—particularly good for a home office space.

Fresh flowers

There's a reason why there are so many beautiful glass vase designs in Sweden. Swedish homes often feature a bouquet of beautiful fresh flowers, a simple way to bring more color and some life into a room. This is particularly true in the darker winter months, when you often need an emotional boost. In December, make room for *julblommor*, Christmas flowers like amaryllis, hyacinth, Christmas begonias, and poinsettias. In January and February, freshly cut tulips are popular, and come springtime it's a celebration of flowers such as daffodils and potted crocuses.

Branches

Bare branches, from whatever trees you have near you, can be featured on their own, or decorated with small lights for a natural feel in the home. If you're pruning trees in the springtime, such as apple trees, keep a few branches and put them in vases or glass jars and wait for the buds to bloom.

Pick a bouquet of wildflowers

There's an unpretentiousness to wildflowers that's celebrated in Swedish homes. When flowers are abloom in summer months, vases on kitchen tables are full of them. Picking wildflowers lets you spend time in nature and bring it indoors, the best of both worlds.

SUSTAINABILITY

As you have read this book, I am certain that you have picked up on a few themes. Equality and the common good is one of them, quite obviously expressed through the Swedish attitude to work and design. The other is sustainability. Perhaps the most important thing about balance and Slow Living is that it represents a more sustainable lifestyle.

Sustainability is a word that gets thrown around a lot. It's co-opted by marketing campaigns to sell more things (the antithesis of sustainability) and it's a catch-all phrase that can refer to everything from our clothes to our food.

But sustainability is important. Not just important, essential. We are currently 7 billion people on this planet, and that's projected to rise to 9.5 billion by 2050. Our impact on our world is significant and growing daily. Consumption of food, water, and energy is increasing at an exponential rate, pushing us to the limits of what our Earth can sustain. In the developed world, these consumption rates are higher. According to a 2012 report "People and the Planet" published by the Royal Society, a child from the developed world consumes thirty to fifty times more water than a child from the developing world. The same discrepancy exists in regards to carbon dioxide emissions, which are up to fifty times higher in high-income countries.

Many of our daily habits and products have impacts far beyond what we see. Our wardrobes have a footprint. For example, it takes more than 2,000 gallons of water to produce one pair of jeans, not to mention the amount of pesticides that go into growing the cotton used to make them. Our consumptive societies are wasteful and come at a social and environmental cost.

In the last few decades we have failed to have a lagom approach towards the environment. We have taken everything that we can—resources and space—and I would argue here that the result is that because of our previous actions, when it comes to the environment, today a lagom approach won't be enough. Instead we need an aggressive approach, particularly from a policy perspective. Sweden, in many ways, is a leader in forward-thinking policy that considers both the wellbeing of the population and the environment, understanding that the two go hand in hand.

The solutions to these problems are not simple, but sustainability is a global issue that requires a multitude of approaches, and many of these start at home. Here is an ideal place for a more lagom attitude. There are many things that we can't give up in our everyday life, like getting to work, for example, but a more lagom approach can help us to adapt our daily routines, such as taking the bus instead of driving to the office. If we all lived more lagom and more balanced—with regards to work, consumption, our homes, and what we eat—we would greatly reduce our overall impact on the planet. If we continue with our extremely consumptive lifestyles we will strip the resources of today, leaving nothing for tomorrow. We cannot push ourselves or our environment to its most extreme limits, and this is why scaling back to a more lagom approach is essential. Living lagom means that the next generation can live lagom too.

There are actions that we can take in our every day to reduce our impact on the world around us:

Consider materials and ingredients
In our wardrobes, in our furniture, in our beauty products, in our cleaning products, even in our food,

materials and ingredients matter. Start looking at what chemicals are involved in making everyday products, from furniture to paint to clothing.

Reduce waste
Many of us have learnt the three Rs—reduce, reuse, and recycle—but to accommodate our desire to regularly consume, we have mainly focused on the third one, recycling. There is a reason why in that list reduce comes first. Reducing our overall daily consumption is essential, which in turn reduces our waste. Consider how many throwaway items make their way into your everyday routine, then see which of those things you can reduce, or remove entirely, from your habits. Bringing a reusable shopping bag to the store has become a habit for many, but what about food packaging? Buying fresh produce and bulk foods can also help to reduce your overall waste.

Reduce food waste
In Europe, 88 billion tons of food goes to waste every year. Part of this happens along the food supply chain, but we can do our part at home to ensure that we are making better use of our food. If you are able to, buy

in smaller batches of food, particularly when it comes to produce. Make meal plans, so that when you go shopping you know exactly what you need to get for the coming week and you don't buy items that will go unused.

Give up bottled water
If we live in places with potable water, disposable plastic water bottles are an unnecessary part of our lives. Make a habit of bringing your own reusable water bottle, and fill it with tap water.

Upcycle
Before throwing something away, consider if it can be repurposed into something new. Old glass jars can be filled with a bouquet of wildflowers for a friendly gift, or used as a unique candleholder. Use an old table as an outdoor table. Felt old sweaters and use the fabric to sew into a blanket, or a pair of mittens.

Mend
Fast fashion and cheap clothes have made it faster and easier to buy something new than to fix something that's a bit worn. In the face of those consumption habits, today

there is a small mending revival, encouraging people to fix their worn clothes instead of dumping them into a trash can. Visible mending—where you see the stitches or the patch that has been used to cover a hole—is turning into an art form, bringing value back to what was once considered old and broken.

Compost

Composting is a way to ensure that our food waste and other organic matter goes back into the natural cycle. There are many types of composting depending on what your needs are, and even if you don't have the garden space to build your own compost facility, many community gardens and cities now offer composting opportunities.

Buy second-hand

Make a habit of seeing what's available second-hand when you are in need of something new for your wardrobe or your home. The result of a culture of excess means that the market is flooded with objects, from clothing to furniture, and if you have the time to spend doing a little research, you can end up with inexpensive, unique objects that deserve a second life.

Buy less

Today there is an assortment of eco-friendly and green products on the market, but the truth is that conscious consumerism won't save us. When you need a pair of jeans, yes, it's an excellent choice to opt for a second-hand pair, or ones made with good textiles and produced in an ethical fashion. But at the same time, we also need to challenge our own perceptions of what we need and how we consume. Buying an increasing number of products that are more ethical and eco-friendly isn't the solution, buying less is. Opting out isn't always fun, but assessing what we need and don't need, and working on minimizing our consumption habits, means that we make room for other, more meaningful things, like experiences.

Teach the next generation

Good habits begin early and if you have children, or spend time with children, make respecting the environment a part of their daily habits. Teach them where their food comes from, talk about topics like waste and consumption. It can be hard to switch to a more lagom approach to living when we're used to a life

of excess, but if it's ingrained in us from the beginning, it's simply part of who we are.

Energy efficiency
There are many small changes that we can incorporate into our lives in order to make our homes more energy efficient. Not only do these things help to reduce our overall energy consumption and impact, but they also result in saving money.

• Install energy-efficient light bulbs like Light Emitting Diode (LED) and Compact Fluorescent Lights (CFL) bulbs.
• Only do laundry when you have a full load, and wash your clothes in cold water.
• Install an energy-efficient showerhead.
• Turn your heat down by a few degrees, and only heat rooms that you are using.
• Fill your kettle with only the amount of water you need for your cup of tea or coffee.
• Turn off the lights in a room when you leave it.

Travel

Travel comes at a significant impact. Air miles alone account for enormous amounts of CO_2 emissions. We don't need to cut out our far-flung adventures entirely, but we can scale back on them, and make more sustainable choices when we are away from home. When it comes to trip planning, consider fewer trips that are longer as opposed to many short trips. When you are travelling, opt for local public transportation. Stay in places that believe in reducing their impact as well. When you are in a new place, discover that place, engage with those who live there, go off the beaten tourist track; make an effort to interact and support the local economy.

Support nature

If you love nature, support it. There's a good chance there's an environmental initiative near you that needs an extra volunteer, or some additional funding. Instead of buying a new eco-friendly item that you don't need, support a good cause.

THE LESSONS OF LAGOM

Sustainability can also relate to the sustainability of our own lives. When we live in the extremes, it's easy to push too hard, leaving us exhausted and depleted of our own resources. A sustainable lifestyle is one that considers our personal health, both mental and physical. We drive too fast, eat too much, work too hard, stress too often. These are all unsustainable activities. We need to slow down, catch up with ourselves. We have to find the balance between all of the aspects of our lives—health, work, family, economy, and environment.

Doing a more lagom amount of everything allows us to find our own personal balance, one that is sustainable in the long term. Living lagom means finding happiness, one that doesn't come from things, or the numbers in a salary, but from a balanced existence. A happiness that is drawn from contentment with the now.

This is the ultimate takeaway from the idea of lagom, that the only way to build a sustainable path forward is if we scale back on our consumption and treat ourselves, our community, and our environment better. We are all able to apply elements of lagom into our everyday lives, all able to find a balance between too much and too little.

Living fast comes with consequences, and we could all use a bit of slowing down. We could all do with embracing the present, enjoying the every day. Finding beauty in simplicity. Ultimately, for me, this is what lagom has come to represent.

There's still room for indulgence, and there's still room for challenging ourselves and pushing hard. But there's also room for slowing down, living a more moderate, minimal life with less impact to ourselves and the world around us. If we can do that, we can work towards building a more conscious culture.

Lagom är bäst.

RESOURCES/BIBLIOGRAPHY

"Better Life Work Balance" Organisation for Economic Co-operation and Development, http://www.oecdbetterlifeindex.org/topics/work–life-balance/

Blumenthal, James A. PhD; Babyak, Michael A. PhD; Moore, Kathleen A. PhD; et al "Effects of Exercise Training on Older Patients With Major Depression" *Arch Intern Med*, 1999.

Booth, Michael. *The Almost Nearly Perfect People.* Jonathan Cape, 2014.

Creagh, Lucy; Kåberg, Helena and Miller Lane, Barbara, *Modern Swedish Design: Three Founding Texts.* New York: The Museum of Modern Art, 2008.

Hampden-Turner, Charles and Trompenaars, Alfons. *The Seven Cultures of Capitalism.* New York: Doubleday, 1993.

Hetter, Katia. "Where Are the World's Happiest Countries?" CNN, http://www.cnn.com/2016/03/16/travel/worlds-happiest-countries-united-nations/

Johansen, Signe. *How to Hygge: The Nordic Secrets to a Happy Life.* New York: St. Martin's Griffin, 2017.

"Living Planet Report 2016" World Wide Fund for Nature, http://wwf.panda.org/about_our_earth/all_publications/lpr_2016/

McFadden, David Revere, editor. *Scandinavian Modern Design 1880-1980.* New York: Henry N. Abrams, 1982.

Merling, Lara. "The United States Trails Other Countries in Life-Work Balance" Center for Economic and Policy Research. http://cepr.net/blogs/cepr-blog/the-united-states-trails-other-countries-in-work–life-balance

Murphy, Keith. *Swedish Design: An Ethnography.* New York: Cornell University Press, 2014.

"OECD Environmental Performance Reviews: Sweden 2014" Organisation for Economic Co-operation and Development, http://www.oecd.org/env/country-reviews/oecd-environmental-performance-reviews-sweden-2014-9789264213715-en.htm

"Parental Leave" Sweden.se, https://sweden.se/quick-facts/parental-leave/

"People and the Planet Report" The Royal Society, 2012.

"Quick Facts, Renewable Energy" Sweden.se, https://sweden.se/quick-facts/renewable-energy/

Shin, Won Sop. "The influence of forest view through a window on job satisfaction and job stress" *Scandinavian Journal of Forest Research*, 2007.

Wilhide, Elizabeth. *Scandinavian Home: A Comprehensive Guide to Mid-Century Modern Scandinavian Designers*. London: Quadrille Publishing, 2008.

"Water Footprint Product Gallery" Water Footprint Network, http://waterfootprint.org/en/resources/interactive-tools/product-gallery/

ACKNOWLEDGMENTS

There are always many people to thank when writing a book; it's rarely a solo process. Here are a few that I couldn't have made *Live Lagom* without:

First and foremost, thank you to my mother Britta Brones, for not only instilling in me a love of Swedish culture, but for reading numerous drafts and providing essential input (as well as access to her extensive Swedish art and design book library) to make this book happen. To everyone at Ebury, in particular Louise McKeever for reaching out to me and giving birth to the idea for this book. To Mikael Parkvall, Michael Booth, Frida Ramstedt, and Pim Sjöström for their input. To my various Swedish friends, including Kerstin Hagberg and Cecilia Blomberg, for all their personal insight. To Kaitlin Ketchum for ongoing advice on all things publishing. And to Luc Revel for photo and editing help as well as the many discussions about the meaning of working towards a more balanced life.